# THE COMING WEALTH TRANSFER

### Believing The Prophecy
### Applying The Principles
### Preparing To Be A Millionaire for God

**Matthew Ashimolowo**

**Reprinted November 2006**
**© 2006 Matthew Ashimolowo**

Published by Mattyson Media an imprint of MAMM
Matthew Ashimolowo Media Ministries

Visit our website: www.pastormatthew.co.uk

**ISBN 1 874646 70 8**

**Bible quotes are from**
New International Version Bible
King James Bible
The New King James Bible
The New Living Translation
The Amplified Bible
The Living Bible
The Message

## Disclaimer

The advice contained in this material might not be suitable for
everyone. The author designed the information to present his
opinion about the subject matter. The reader must carefully inves-
tigate all aspects of any business decision before committing him -
or herself. The author obtained the information contained therein
from sources he believes to be reliable and from his own personal
experience, but he neither implies nor intends any guarantee of
accuracy. The author is not in the business of giving legal, accounting, or any other type of professional advice. Should the reader
need such advice, he or she must seek services from a competent
professional. The author particularly disclaims any liabilities, loss
or risk taken by individuals who directly or indirectly act on the
information contained herein. The author believes the advice presented here is sound, but readers cannot hold him responsible for
either the actions they take or the result of those actions.

# CONTENTS

## BELIEVING THE PROPHECIES..........................5

Introduction..............................................................7
What Kind Of Wealth Will Be Transferred?..................19

## APPLYING THE PRINCIPLES...........................39

The Purpose Of The Wealth Transfer............................41
The Strategies For The Wealth Transfer........................51
Developing The Mindset For Wealth Creation.............83

## EIGHT CIRCLES OF WEALTH
## CREATION...............................................................103

Knowledge...............................................................111
Commitment.............................................................119
Investment...............................................................123
Portfolio Management...............................................151
Wealth.....................................................................161
Reinvestment...........................................................173
Multi-Generational Wealth.......................................179
Giving.....................................................................187

## ESTABLISHING YOUR FINANCIAL
## FUTURE...................................................................229

Values, Vision and Volume........................................231

## CONCLUSION........................................................253

# BELIEVING THE PROPHECIES

# INTRODUCTION

The opening statement of the Bible, "In the beginning, God created the heaven and the earth" - Genesis 1:1 and the statement of David when he said, "He owns the cattle upon a thousand hills" - Psalm 50:10 immediately present to us a universe wholly owned and created by God Almighty.

This God has created a world of kingdoms, starting with the Kingdom of God, followed by the angelic kingdom, the atmospheric kingdom, the plant kingdom, the animal kingdom, the atomic kingdom, the sub-atomic kingdom and the human kingdom.

It was the promulgation of the first, the Kingdom of God, that necessitated the coming of Christ, reconciling men to God and proclaiming the Kingdom of God.

Jesus also taught us that when people become born again, they become part of the Kingdom of God. Every kingdom has its ambassadors, economy, protocol, statutes and laws etc.

The function of the Church on earth is that it is an extension of the Kingdom of God. Not only is it an extension of the Kingdom of God, its members are citizens of that Kingdom. They play a role of citizens and representatives of the Kingdom. However, the buoyancy of the kingdom you represent determines the respect and impact you make.

In this 21st century, there are questions to be asked. If the Church is the ambassador of Christ,

**1.** Why are there not many miracles to show that it is an extension of a Kingdom of power?

**2.** Why is there not enough demonstration of the resurrection power that rose Jesus from the dead?

*And if the Spirit of him who raised Jesus from the dead is living in you, he who raised Christ from the dead will also give life to*

*your mortal bodies through his Spirit, who lives in you.*
*Romans 8:11*

**3.** Why is the Church struggling financially to meet its needs if it is representing the richest Kingdom?

Looking at it closely, we will notice that essentially, in its attempt to reach the 21st century man, the Church has gone on radio and television. However, 99.9 per cent of these various institutions are wholly owned by individuals and governments, most of them not holding the views, convictions and ethos which the Church represents.

So the Church which is supposed to be the most potent, richest body representing the greatest King, God of Heaven, has to operate on a shoe-string budget, using the tools of those who do not believe in her philosophy to do her work.

Part of this challenge stems from what the Church had taught in the past concerning finance and prosperity. In its attempt to divert people's attention from worldliness it has ended up creating an atmosphere where people shun any financial blessing, focus only on going to heaven, consider abundance as illegitimate and bad, and misinterpret statements of Jesus like when He said it is easier for a camel to go through a needle's eye than for a rich man to make heaven.

The majority of the body of Christ globally has had to depend on handouts from various organisations, including government agencies, to be able to carry out its operation.

The experience of the Church does not add up because it does not sit properly with the promise of the scripture that says, "He brought us out of our past experience and into a wealthy place."

*You let men ride over our heads; we went through fire and water but you brought us to a place of abundance. Psalm 66:12*

Peter said, "We have been invited to an inheritance and the church is not manifesting it.

*And into an inheritance that can never perish spoil or fade-kept in heaven for you. 1 Peter 1:4*

In the past 40 years major ministers and ministries have been speaking of the coming wealth transfer. This includes the likes of Dr Oral Roberts, Kenneth Copeland and Dr Kenneth E. Hagin. In more recent times, the voices of people outside of the Word of Faith Movement have been added to this prophecy. C. Peter Wagner indicated that in several meetings and places where he has been, such prophecies had been coming forth and that this great wealth transfer will take place through the evolution of four kinds of people within the body of Christ.

A new generation of:

**1.** Wealth producers

**2.** Managers

**3.** Distributors

**4.** The Generals of God who will use the wealth for the advancement of the Kingdom of God

In this 21st century, everything happening around us makes this prophecy believable, acceptable and necessary for progress.

The Kingdom of God must be advanced.

Yes, it advances on supernatural power when the Gospel is proclaimed. However imagine the fact that what we see on television, hear on radio or receive as Gospel tracts, books or literature are only a fraction of what may be called the Gospel.

How many young men and women, faithful in their calling, have not been able to impact their world because of financial limitation!

*Now there lived in that city a man poor but wise and he saved the*
*city by his wisdom. But nobody remembered that poor man.*
*Ecclesiastes 9:15*

The Kingdom of God is supposed to permeate the whole of the earth's system.

The best medium has to be the use of timely technology for the timeless truth. That does not come cheap.

Furthermore, Jesus said to us that in this world we would have a hundred fold.

*And everyone who has left houses or brothers or sisters or father or mother or children or fields for my sake will receive a hundred times as much and will inherit eternal life. Matthew 19:29*

That verse is nothing less than a 100 per cent and possibly a 100 per cent of all that we need to do the work, to make an impact and to stand out as Christ's emissaries on earth.

The third reason why this prophecy is imminent and acceptable is based on the scripture which says, "The kingdom of this world has become the Kingdom of our God."

I am personally convinced that this can include the control of the monetary system of this world. It has been for too long in the hands of the devil whereas God said the silver and gold belong to Him.

*The silver is mine and the gold is mine declares the LORD Almighty. Haggai 2:8*

The Church is so far away from this runaway train called the monetary system of the world. However, the One who is behind the Church makes all things beautiful.

The final premise upon which I would want to base the argument is the fact that the Church will be taken home with a trumpet sound. It shows in effect that its departure is with a BANG! Not a minor 'pop' sound. So the latter days of the Church are going to be the most glorious.

Contrary to the negative publicity of those who like to look at the Church and say it is now no longer making an impact and has fewer people, it is making greater impact and having more people coming to the Lord. There are more people saved today than at any time in the history of the Church.

Some people on reading would laugh at the thought that a wealth transfer is on the horizon, that the financial topography of the Church will Change with the Church being involved.

This will start with a supernatural intervention of God. He spoke it, that there would be a wealth transfer.

*I will give you the treasures of darkness riches stored in secret places so that you may know that I am the LORD the God of Israel who summons you by name. Isaiah 45:3*

The supernatural intervention of God will also be accompanied by supernatural wisdom. He will give the insight for possessing all possessions.

*Any enterprise is built by wise planning, becomes strong through common sense, and profits wonderfully by keeping abreast of the facts. Proverbs 24:2-4*

This transfer of wealth does not mean that God will take major corporations, companies and the incredible wealth of the world and put it in the hand of people who cannot handle such stewardship.

In the parable of the talents, Jesus reveals to us the fact that God recognises wise investors who compound the interests and profits, and therefore increases the responsibility He gives to them.

I am convinced that this wealth transfer will only come into the hand of those who are prepared, who have stewarded, studied the system of the world and are open to the supernatural doings of God.

The supernatural wealth transfer that the scripture presents to us has nothing to do with your country of origin, its history, upheavals, economic revolution, blessing or setback.

It is a subject of the breakthrough of God. It has nothing to do with age. Those who are open to receiving this wealth will do, whether young or old.

The destiny of the Church and those who make up the Church is independent of the condition of their birth. The fact that you were born with a silver spoon in your mouth or in the atmosphere of lack has very little to do with this.

Yet, God cannot do anything except with the cooperation of the individual whom He will use in the process of wealth creation.

Just as the realities of the nations we live in, the financial condition the Church has found in itself and the individual plights we face were created by us, that is how God will empower individuals also to bring the solutions.

*But remember the LORD your God for it is he who gives you the ability to produce wealth and so confirms his covenant which he swore to your forefathers as it is today. Deuteronomy 8:18*

## TIMING

It is safe to say that with all the prophecies that have gone forth we must be close to the season for such transfer. The conditions prevailing when such transfers took place in the Old Testament seem to be with us again.

Our first example is the Exodus of the Israelites out of Egypt. On the night before their departure, God told them to go and spoil the Egyptians - that is to take from them what was the instrument of their wealth, their gold and other valuables.

The favour of the Lord was so manifest that the Egyptians willingly handed it over. It was not possible for a nation constituting ex-slaves to have been able to carry out a project the Lord was to reveal to them later in the wilderness, i.e. the building of the tabernacle which required a lot of gold, without them having been empowered prior to that time.

In effect the wealth transfer which took place in Egypt was for use in the wilderness to build a temple for God.

The second time we make reference to was when there was famine in Israel and there was hardly enough to feed on. Elijah showed up in the horizon and prophesied a sudden availability of abundance.

This story goes to show that wealth transfer will meet the ministerial and global need for evangelism which the Church has. It will also be available for the economic need of the body of Christ and members in particular.

The timings of God will also require that the appropriate birth engine for the effective running of this wealth transfer should be in place.

The first of these birth engines is the government of the Church - that is the spiritual atmosphere and the body of Christ being conducive for all the five gifts of Ephesians 4:11 to operate.

The second birth engine is those with the gifts of administration. Essentially in the words of C. Peter Wagner, four kinds of people need to be in place:

## 1. The providers -

Just like the Egyptians who provided for the needs of Israel, these providers need not be Christians. However they will be used as conduits for passing the wealth into the hands of believers.

## 2. The managers -

Those who have the skills and ability to take what has been provided and generate a multiplication of it. This fits into the story of the talents where the Lord Jesus commended the managers who compounded the interest and benefit of the talents given to them.

## 3. The distributors -

These are men, women, institutions and governments that will be Church-friendly, whom God will use as a networking bridge to the fourth group and to make the funds available.

## 4. Field marshals -

Certain men and women whom, in the words of C. Peter Wagner again, could be described as "Field marshals" who have the capacity to look beyond their own immediate need and consider what has been put in their hand as instruments for reaching, planting, evangelising and transformation.

Not all of these four steps are strong at the moment.

The field marshals are in place and the provision is. With time, the appropriate managers and distributors will evolve.

One of the aims of this book is to challenge the Christian to the reality that we can combine the prophecy of God's

Word with the principles of fund management and achieve the Mind of Christ.

These two truths presented are applicable in many nations of the world. The country of our birth is irrelevant in this matter. God is able to break through irrespective of where we find ourselves. He is able to give the strength, ability and capacity to make it happen through hard work and the management of what has been provided.

*Dishonest money dwindles away but he who gathers money little by little makes it grow. Proverbs 13:11*

*The sluggard craves and gets nothing but the desires of the diligent are fully satisfied. Proverbs 13:4*

*But remember the LORD your God for it is he who gives you the ability to produce wealth and so confirms his covenant which he swore to your forefathers as it is today. Deuteronomy 8:18*

# WHAT KIND OF WEALTH WILL BE TRANSFERRED?

**A**s I sit down to write, this morning of April 16th 2006, the lost condition of the world dawns very strongly upon me. There are 6.5 billion people on earth, the majority of whom do not know Christ as their Lord and Saviour, neither do they have a personal relationship with Him.

I am not saying the Church has lost ground: however we are even at a point where here in Europe, the Church, including evangelicals, are calling for a dialogue with certain religions as if accepting defeat and believing that all roads lead to God.

This of course does not negate the Word of God which makes it very clear that Jesus is the only way, the truth and the life.

*Jesus answered "I am the way and the truth and the life. No one comes to the Father except through me. John 14:6*

The Church's inability to reach the world, to my knowledge, stems very much from its own theology and attitude to the subject of finance. For a long time, the Church belittled the necessity for financial wealth in the life of its members. This of course probably accounts for the meagre offering the majority of churches end up collecting.

So while we plan our evangelistic meetings around basic tracts and streets meetings, the decision makers and the voices of the nation whom we ought to reach, among others, are locked up in their beautiful air-conditioned cars, homes and offices.

The majority of the Church lacks the finance with which to use timely technology to preach the timeless truth. This statement about the condition of the Church seems like a generalisation; however one must acknowledge that there are exceptions and a few places where certain meetings, organisations, evangelistic programmes, church outreaches, and TV programmes have been done with great excellence. But they are few and far between.

The Church continues in this state when a tremendous treasury belonging to the Father of the Church is ready and available; however, our attitude has stopped us from tapping into it.

## 1. Wealth is an armoury

It is the tool by which we can do spiritual warfare. If we must fight today's enemy of the cross we must use a tool equal to or greater than him. Here in Europe, on the Sky Digital television, although there are close to 300 TV channels, only about nine could be considered to be Christian TV stations while the channels that represent various sexual tendencies are more than 50.

Owning the licence to run a TV station comes in the hundreds of thousands of euros. That is why the scripture clearly indicates that wealth is an instrument of protection.

> *The wealth of the rich is their fortified city but poverty is the ruin of the poor. Proverbs 10:15*

It is a defensive weapon against those who want to encroach on the good news of Jesus Christ.

## 2. The body of Christ is supposed to be a depository of God for His blessings

God said to Abraham, "I will bless you."

> *I will make you into a great nation and I will bless you; I will make your name great and you will be a blessing. Genesis 12:2*

However, God does not put His blessing irrationally, just about anywhere. There must be an attitude of faith and a commitment to use such wealth for His glory. If you do not desire to be blessed it will not come. No man who came to the meeting of Jesus was healed without a desire for it.

## 3. A storehouse

The book of Malachi describes what God wants to give the Church. Not pockets of offerings and little gifts but a storehouse where great things could be transferred into for the Church to be able to use to make a major impact.

*Bring the whole tithe into the storehouse, that there may be food in my house. Test me in this," says the LORD Almighty, "and see if I will not throw open the floodgates of heaven and pour out so much blessing that you will not have room enough for it.*
*Malachi 3:10*

There are three levels of blessings indicated in the book of Deuteronomy 28.

## The works of your hand

*The LORD will open the heavens the storehouse of his bounty to send rain on your land in season and to bless all the work of your hands. Deuteronomy 28:12a*

## Your basket

*Your basket and your kneading trough will be blessed.*
*Deuteronomy 28:5*

## Your storehouse

*The LORD will send a blessing on your barns and on everything you put your hand to. The LORD your God will bless you in the land he is giving you. Deuteronomy 28:8*

Each one is a graduation from one level to the other, requiring a different faith level and vision to be able to access such provision.

## 4. A collection point

God's wealth constantly searches for a people or organisation, individuals or nations under God who will become a barn, a collection point to store up and use what He is about to provide.

*Is there yet any seed left in the barn? Until now the vine and the fig tree the pomegranate and the olive tree have not borne fruit. 'From this day on I will bless you.' Haggai 2:19*

Such provision is certainly not for personal aggrandisement but for the furtherance of the Gospel and making the good news heard in all corners. It is to be able to use it to establish the purpose of God.

## WHAT WEALTH WILL GOD SHIFT TO THE CHURCH IN THESE LAST DAYS?

## 1. Treasures

We are given various descriptions of these treasures coming to the Body of Christ.

## A. The treasures of darkness

*I will give you the treasures of darkness, riches stored in secret places so that you may know that I am the LORD the God of Israel who summons you by name. Isaiah 45:3*

We must literally take the word darkness or hidden riches in this verse to be referring to the fact that it is kept stored up until the days when the eye of the Church is illuminated.

*I pray also that the eyes of your heart may be enlightened in order that you may know the hope to which he has called you the riches of his glorious inheritance in the saints. Ephesians 1:18*

So the Church will know what has been stored up for her, draw such resource and use it for the purpose for which He established His Church.

## B. Sealed up treasures

*"Have I not kept this in reserve and sealed it in my vaults? Deuteronomy 32:34*

Sealed up in the realms of the spirit with the mark of the sovereign God are great treasures that are yet to be unleashed on the earth. Twenty five years ago, nobody knew of the wealth that would come through information technology and just when we think that we have seen the best, the last and the greatest, God keeps permitting new treasures to be unleashed on the earth.

On a funnier side, maybe because the Church did not trust in the God who called Himself the One who opens doors that no man can shut.

*I know your deeds. See, I have placed before you an open door that no one can shut. I know that you have little strength, yet you have kept my word and have not denied my name. Revelation 3:8*

When the Church did not believe Him to open great doors, He gave people like Microsoft, the Windows!

## C. Treasures in the sand

Anyone who watched films like Lawrence of Arabia never knew that hidden under the sands of the Arabian lands was the black gold now known as crude oil. That treasure has since empowered and enriched people of the Mediterranean peninsula; however, my conviction is that since this promise is to the Church, there is still yet to be unleashed another treasure hidden in the sands, waiting for the Church to come into the fullness of its revelation.

## D. Treasures of kings

*As the LORD had declared Nebuchadnezzar removed all the treasures from the temple of the LORD and from the royal palace and took away all the gold articles that Solomon king of Israel had made for the temple of the LORD. 2 Kings 24:13*

It was the practice in Bible times and even up to the Roman Empire for kings to hide their treasures under the earth in the fear of another invading army.

2 Kings 24:13 makes us understand that such treasures will one day be put in the hands of the Body of Christ. The treasures taken out of kings' houses, hidden under the sand in various places are coming to the Church.

## E. Treasures in the field

*But ten of them said to Ishmael "Don't kill us! We have wheat and barley oil and honey hidden in a field." So he let them alone and did not kill them with the others. Jeremiah 41:8*

In the course of this transfer, the day is coming when God will give the Church ideas, breakthrough concepts in the field of agriculture that will feed the world that is living in hunger today. That in itself will become a channel by which the Gospel is being preached to the majority of the world that is still obstinate and hardened away from the Gospel.

## F. Treasures of the East

*On coming to the house, they saw the child with his mother Mary, and they bowed down and worshiped him. Then they opened their treasures and presented him with gifts of gold and of incense and of myrrh. Matthew 2:11*

*Early the next morning Abraham took some food and a skin of water and gave them to Hagar. He set them on her shoulders and then sent her off with the boy. She went on her way and wandered in the desert of Beersheba. Genesis 21:14*

My understanding of biblical prophecy and the law of

reciprocity makes me to believe that just as Abraham sent Ishmael away to the East with blessings, the sons of Ishmael came back bearing gifts for the baby Jesus. That journey will still be repeated as treasures are brought from the East to the Body of Christ, to use for the proclamation of the Gospel.

## 2. Hidden riches

Isaiah talks of hidden riches of secret places.

> *I will give you the treasures of darkness, riches stored in secret places so that you may know that I am the LORD the God of Israel who summons you by name. Isaiah 45:3*

Hidden because the time has not come. Hidden because the Church has not matured. Hidden because we are not ready for the wealth transfer. Hidden because the Church holds a theology that precludes her from appreciating, embracing and using such wealth.

## 3. Unstewarded favour

> *You will arise and have compassion on Zion for it is time to show favor to her; the appointed time has come. Psalm 102:13*

Favour is God's way of fast tracking a man from the back of the queue to the front. It is God giving you in one day of favour what you could not get in one year of labour. It is the supernatural breakthrough that causes doors to open for you even in high places, making laws, rules, regulations and statutes that were established to hinder people like you, to be revoked, repealed or suspended because your season of blessing has come.

It was favour that gave Joseph access in the house of the General Potiphar. It was the kind of favour that gave him the right to sit in the ruling cabinet of the Egyptian Empire though he was a foreigner, uneducated, unschooled, an ex-prisoner, ex-house keeper, ex-shepherd. Favour looks past your weak and indicting curriculum vitae.

## 4. Inheritance

The greatest motivation for taking Israel out of the land of slavery was God painting a picture of their inheritance waiting for them while they slaved away in Egypt. A picture of a land that flowed with milk and honey, a land where the stone was like iron, a land where they would have plenty and abundance was enough to make them ready to face the consequence, and possess their possession.

God's intention for Israel, just like the Church was that they might be His holy nation, His picture to the world of what a relationship with God could be.

*You will bring them in and plant them on the mountain of your inheritance- the place O LORD you made for your dwelling the sanctuary O Lord your hands established. Exodus 15:17*

*The land is to be allotted to them as an inheritance based on the number of names. To a larger group give a larger inheritance, and to a smaller group a smaller one; each is to receive its inheritance according to the number of those listed. Numbers 26:53-54*

Israel though, had a part to play. They were to know that, yes this wealth transfer shall not just be merely preserved on a platter of gold without them taking their stand, believing and fighting for it. God gave them the responsibility to drive out the squatters.

*To drive out before you nations greater and stronger than you and to bring you into their land to give it to you for your inheritance as it is today. Deuteronomy 4:38*

The Church has an inheritance, earthly and eternal. The eternal is indicated in the words of Peter.

*And into an inheritance that can never perish spoil or fade kept in heaven for you. 1 Peter 1:4*

Having an inheritance though does not mean you have possessed it unless actual steps are taken. At different times in my journey here in the United Kingdom, the newspaper will feature a person who lives the life of a punk, sleeping under bridges, wearing dirty clothes while on the other hand, two to three hours drive from where he lives under the bridge the same person was supposed to be an heir to a 3,000 acre estate and an inheritance of millions of pounds. So they were living in poverty, sometimes dying through drug overdose, while millions waited for them.

## 5. Stolen property restored

*Men do not despise a thief if he steals to satisfy his hunger when he is starving. Yet if he is caught, he must pay sevenfold, though it costs him all the wealth of his house. Proverbs 6:30-31*

There is a failure of the Church to occupy its proper place, possess her possession and use such possession for the proclamation of the Gospel. However, once she wakes up it shall be to an inheritance that was stolen but must be restored sevenfold.

## 6. Benefits

Psalm 68:19 describes God as One who wants to daily load the believer with blessings - even the benefits of salvation. This is replicated in Psalms 103:2 and 116:12.

*Praise the LORD, O my soul, and forget not all his benefits-*
*Psalm 103:2*

*How can I repay the LORD for all his goodness to me?*
*Psalm 116:12*

The Hebrew and Greek word for Salvation both convey the concept that it is more than being saved from sin. It includes deliverance, favour, blessing and benefits.

The majority of the Church today celebrates a one legged salvation that only talks of being saved from sin but fails to refer to the fact that we were delivered from something to be brought into a blessing.

*You let men ride over our heads; we went through fire and water but you brought us to a place of abundance. Psalm 66:12*

## 7. Divine ideas for wealth creation

The Church will need to fully wake up to the promise of Deuteronomy 8:18 which says, "He it is who gives you power to create wealth."

This creative ability is where the greatest wealth transfer of the future lies. Somewhere between your two ears could lie the greatest concept, idea or insight that will change the financial well-being of your family and your ability to impact the Kingdom of God.

Our world has become a world of creative domination. From the internet to the computer, from the iPod to the cell phone. These are all products of creative ideas.

*"For my thoughts are not your thoughts, neither are your ways my ways," declares the LORD. "As the heavens are higher than the earth, so are my ways higher than your ways and my thoughts than your thoughts. As the rain and the snow come down from heaven, and do not return to it without watering the earth and making it bud and flourish, so that it yields seed for the sower and bread for the eater, so is my word that goes out from my mouth: It will not return to me empty, but will accomplish what I desire and achieve the purpose for which I sent it. You will go out in joy and be led forth in peace; the mountains and hills will burst into song before you, and all the trees of the field will clap their hands. Instead of the thornbush will grow the pine tree, and instead of briers the myrtle will grow. This will be for the LORD's renown, for an everlasting sign, which will not be destroyed."*
*Isaiah 55:8-13*

The possibility is there that the Church which really is its membership have had great ideas; however, because we have played down the importance of these things we may have missed great opportunities to raise world champion believers who are using their ideas to bless the world and also create the wealth for preaching the Gospel.

Some great ideas have slipped through the hands of those who had it. The Mail on Sunday, a British newspaper on 16th April 2006 listed six people who had great ideas but never really made much of it and never profited from it.

The first one was J K Rowlings' book, Harry Potter and the Philosopher's Stone. Though I do not subscribe to it, yet we must quote it for the sake of illustration. That book was submitted by her literary agent to publishers. The first one turned it down within a day. The remaining 12 publishers turned it down. Bloomsbury took it on and the rest was history.

Decca records turned down the Beatles in 1962 because they sounded like another group called, "The Shadows," only to be taken on by Palofone, they went on to become the world's most famous band.

In 1967 Roward Kearns invented the intermittent car windscreen wiper. He took his argument to some companies like Ford. Of course they tried to bypass him, using his idea for which he later claimed money from them.

Nicola Tesla, a Serbian immigrant to America, invented

the modern electric power system, fluorescent bulbs, neon lights, the speedometer and the basics behind radio, radar and microwave ovens and sold all for the paltry sum of $260,000. Today, trillions of dollars have been made with this one man's idea.

Software genius Gary Gildall invented the first operating systems for a personal computer. However, when invited for a meeting with IBM, he went flying. Bill Gates went on to sell his own MS-Dos. The rest is history.

Kane Kramer, a British gentleman designed and sketched out the first iPod in 1979 but did nothing with it. Today the iPod has taken over the world. He remains a store man at a furniture showroom in Hertfordshire, England.

Ideas rule the world and the last great ones are coming to the church.

## 8. Prosperity

We have put this on its own, as the one way God is going to transfer wealth because it has several properties.

Prosperity firstly is advancement. It is the improvement and development of your personal life, vision, dream and capacity. Prosperity comes in your direction with abundance, giving you a great starting point but not an end. It is a by-product of an effective management of whatever God provides.

Prosperity is like a river current. As you keep it flowing, it is wise to be where the prosperity is flowing to.

*Do not be overwicked, and do not be a fool- why die before your time? Ecclesiastes 7:17*

*May there be peace within your walls and security within your citadels. Psalm 122:7*

*Do not add to his words, or he will rebuke you and prove you a liar. Proverbs 30:6*

It is one great method God wants to use to spread His Kingdom from corner to corner of our planet.

*Proclaim further: This is what the LORD Almighty says: 'My towns will again overflow with prosperity and the LORD will again comfort Zion and choose Jerusalem.' Zechariah 1:17*

## 9. Supernatural debt cancellation

While the Church teaches and attacks the subject of prosperity in the Body of Christ in a lot of places in western Europe and America, yet the majority of the membership of the Church live in houses with large mortgages spanning 25 years to pay.

This is a debt that hangs around their neck and sometimes is passed down to the children. A good number of church members live and swim in an ocean of debt. Because of credit facilities available they drive a car that is not really theirs, and they buy carpets, and furniture that are not really theirs. They belong to the finance company.

Even the word 'mortgage' comes from two words: mortification and gage. To mortify is to kill. So mortgage means the measure of your death. Yet God is a debt cancelling God.

We know He is a debt cancelling God. When the prophets went out to cut wood, an axe head fell into the river - that instrument of commerce with which wood was chopped to feed a family. God caused the axe head to swim again.

When the widow who was left broke, busted and disgusted by her husband who probably held views against the personal prosperity of God's people, it required a debt cancelling God to bring her and her children out of it.

*She went and told the man of God, and he said, "Go, sell the oil and pay your debts. You and your sons can live on what is left."*
*2 Kings 4:7*

## 10. Properties

In my experience as a man who has lived in the city of London for 22 years, one of the greatest ways God has transferred and is transferring wealth to His people in these last days is through land and houses.
God is always interested in putting land in people's hands.

*The LORD had said to Abram, "Leave your country, your people and your father's household and go to the land I will show you". Genesis 12:1*

*The LORD appeared to Abram and said, "To your offspring I will give this land." So he built an altar there to the LORD, who had appeared to him. Genesis 12: 7*

There was a time in 1990 when I used to do a prayer walk into the heart of the business district of the city of London. This was usually early in the morning. My observation most times was that a good number of people I knew in church walked into the city early in the morning to clean buildings and as the morning broke and day became clear those who were to occupy these offices to conduct businesses were not exactly church people. The exchange of traffic was very clear.

My members and particularly the community I was reaching were the ones cleaning the offices for others to occupy. I began to pray for God to give me something that could cause a transfer, a change to the community in which I served. Not long after that I began to teach the members of our church how to pay off their debts, how to pay off their mortgages and buy more properties.

At the time of writing this book, probably more than half of our congregation own their own properties. So God intends in the last days to transfer wealth through land, cities (Deuteronomy 6:10), houses (Deuteronomy 6:11) and even harvests which we get from such land.

Later in this book I will show how in the course of teaching we have seen people come into wealth through land and houses or even greater than that, I will share testimonies which will indicate to you that clearly, the great wealth transfer has already begun.

This chapter on what wealth God will transfer to the Church is not by any way exhaustive. We have not seen all that God can do as yet. There is still a great surprise for the Body of Christ. However, God wants people to be ready when He begins this process of transfer.

# APPLYING THE PRINCIPLES

# THE PURPOSE OF THE WEALTH TRANSFER

**W**henever a people do not fully understand the purpose of a thing, they are likely to use it to solve the immediate problem which seems to come up.

Nothing is more beautiful and romantic than when provision and purpose kiss, when they both meet at the point of need. God has a reason for the great wealth transfer coming.

Paramount among the reasons why this great wealth transfer will take place is world evangelisation. Touching the lives of lost men with the good news of Jesus Christ, using every financial opportunity God provides to be able to do ministry effectively.

Thank God for the Hudson Taylors who went to China and the several missionaries who gave their lives in Africa, Latin America, Asia, and the Middle East etc. However, also imagine the fact that by reason of television, radio, the internet, and the cell phone one can reach millions if not billions in a matter of seconds.

As one who ministers on God TV, it is really very humbling for me to consider the fact that that particular channel reaches 214 nations. This means in effect that I am ministering to millions of people in all these nations. I do not know how I could ever visit 214 nations in my lifetime.

The use of such wealth for the proclamation of the Gospel is a natural laying up in store of treasures in heaven as indicated by the Lord Jesus in Matthew 6:20.

*But store up for yourselves treasures in heaven where moth and rust do not destroy and where thieves do not break in and steal.*
*Matthew 6:20*

The souls that are saved for eternity are treasures which end up stored up in heaven. There will be wealth transfer because the presence of poverty is a proof that the curses of scripture are still alighting on the believer.

*Christ redeemed us from the curse of the law by becoming
a curse for us, for it is written: "Cursed is everyone who is
hung on a tree." He redeemed us in order that the blessing
given to Abraham might come to the Gentiles through
Christ Jesus, so that by faith we might receive the
promise of the Spirit.  Galatians 3:13-14*

*However, if you do not obey the LORD your God and do not
carefully follow all his commands and decrees I am giving you
today, all these curses will come upon you and overtake you: You
will be cursed in the city and cursed in the country. Your basket
and your kneading trough will be cursed.
Deuteronomy 28:15-17*

It is very difficult to be able to touch the world in our
own brokenness and emptiness, if we ourselves have not
had our financial challenges resolved.

Wealth transfer will aid the proclamation of the Gospel.
It will help us to feed the hungry.

*"Then the King will say to those on his right, 'Come, you who are
blessed by my Father; take your inheritance, the kingdom prepared
for you since the creation of the world. For I was hungry and you
gave me something to eat, I was thirsty and you gave me something
to drink, I was a stranger and you invited me in, I needed clothes
and you clothed me, I was sick and you looked after me, I was in
prison and you came to visit me.' "Then the righteous will answer
him, 'Lord, when did we see you hungry and feed you, or thirsty
and give you something to drink? When did we see you a stranger
and invite you in, or needing clothes and clothe you? When did we
see you sick or in prison and go to visit you?' "The King will*

*reply, 'I tell you the truth, whatever you did for one of the least of these brothers of mine, you did for me.' Matthew 25:34-40*

A great wealth transfer will help us to achieve matters that have eternal consequences. Every waking moment, every minute of each day over 70 people cross into eternity, Christ-less and hopeless. Many of them have not heard the Gospel of Christ in spite of the proliferation of churches and ministries.

The church desperately needs to experience a wealth transfer to be able to effectively carry out its ministry. The purpose of the great wealth transfer is to fulfil the Word of God when Jesus said, "In this world you will have a hundred fold."

*"I tell you the truth," Jesus replied, "no one who has left home or brothers or sisters or mother or father or children or fields for me and the gospel will fail to receive a hundred times as much in this present age (homes, brothers, sisters, mothers, children and fields- and with them, persecutions) and in the age to come, eternal life. Mark 10:29-30*

One thing with God is that He will not break a sacred promise. Wealth transfer will help the Church to carry out the purpose of God on earth. There are people worshiping under trees. What a beauty it would be if individuals would go round the world just erecting church buildings for such people.

While I do not know the faith of the top ten wealthiest men on the earth quoted by Forbes magazine, I am tempted to reach a conclusion that they would not have a personal relationship with the Lord Jesus Christ.

Were they to have and were they to have an understanding that any wealth given to them was to be used for the proclamation of the Gospel and for touching of lives, imagine what Bill Gates' $48 billion, Warren Buffett's $28 billion dollars or Lakshmi Mittal's $32 dollars could do in changing the world for Christ.

The great wealth transfer will aid the Church to help the needy. The best way to reach any man is to minister to him on all levels - spirit, soul and body.

What is the use preaching the Gospel to a hungry man when he primarily wants you to provide shelter for him or food for his stomach? Today, the Church, in its own little way is involved in showing compassion to the world. This is buttressed by ministries like Compassion International, World Vision, Christian Aid, Samaritans Purse, the Salvation Army etc, who all have their roots in the Church and the Gospel.

Certainly this list is not exhaustive and every local church is trying to be part of the solution to the crisis in our world today. But the great wealth transfer to the Body of Christ will make her even more relevant, particularly in places where the Gospel is more resisted. No man can resist the arm of love and compassion shown them.

The purpose of the great wealth transfer will also be to correct the receiver mentality which many in the Body of Christ have developed. While they belittle and criticise increase and prosperity, yet they desire to receive from those who seem to have it.

We have constantly used the word 'transfer' in this book and one would wonder why God would want to take it from the hands of the ones who have lived for it or worked hard for it, who do not know Christ. It is my conviction that the day is coming when one of the reasons for the great wealth transfer is in order for the church to administer the wealth of the world for the good of the community.

> "Surplus wealth is a sacred trust which its possessor is bound to administer in his lifetime for the good of the community." - **Andrew Carnegie**

The billionaires quoted earlier would not use their wealth for the advancement of the Gospel. They would not even think of the need for Gospel TV and radio stations, or the building of church buildings for believers to occupy.

The great wealth transfer will happen so the Church can apply it wisely.

> "The gratification of wealth is not found in mere possessions or in lavish expenditure, but in its wise application." - **Miguel de Cervantes.**

The competition among the world sometimes gives the impression that it is all about numbers and the desire to outdo the other. There will be a great wealth transfer because the Church understands that the earth is the Lord's and the fullness thereof.

*The earth is the LORD's and everything in it the world and all who live in it; Psalm 24:1*

The Church understands how to use what God will provide.

> "No one should be rich except those who understand it." **Johann Goethe**

Jesus told us that when we use this wealth to preach the good news of the Kingdom there will be other increases which will follow. This makes the purpose of the wealth transfer to be fulfilled when truly we lay our treasure in heaven.

> "You cannot hold on to anything good, you must be continually giving and getting. You cannot hold on to your seed. You must sow it and reap anew. You cannot hold on to riches. You must use them and get other riches in turn." - **Robert Collier**

It is not for hoarding, it is to be used to touch the world.

> "Not he who has much is rich but he who gives much." **Eric Fromm**
>
> ..........................................
>
> "Riches do not consist in the possession of treasures but in the use made of them." - **Napoleon Bonaparte**

A believer therefore must know his personal purposes and know why he wants to be blessed, why he wants the wealth transfer, why he wants more. Because once you have more, if you do not have the inner strength, the maturity to handle the blessings of God, several people have been changed and the prosperity of fools ends up destroying them. Once they do not realise that for anyone who is given abundance, it is a gift from God.

> "Possessions are a gift from God, they are not inherently evil nor are possessions irrelevant to God. If they are, why then the commandment, 'Thou shalt not steal'." - **Dr Laura Schlessinger**
>
> ......................................
>
> "Wealth is not in making money but in making the man while he is making money." - **John Wicker**

Furthermore Winston Churchill said, "We make a living by what we get but we make a life by what we give."

Much has been said about the purpose of the great wealth transfer as it relates to the preaching of the Gospel. However, we must understand also that wise application includes God providing for members of the Body of Christ in order for them to enjoy.

> *Command those who are rich in this present world not to be arrogant nor to put their hope in wealth which is so uncertain but to put their hope in God who richly provides us with everything for our enjoyment. 1 Timothy 6:17*

God is not against your comfort or well-being.

> "Wealth is well-known to be a great comforter." - **Plato**
>
> ......................................
>
> "Wealth is not his that has it but his that enjoys it." - **Benjamin Franklin**

When God therefore gives the believer insight that will cause a wealth transfer or when God causes doors to open that will make this happen, God makes such wealth available to believers. So while he is busy using it for the Gospel, he is also enjoying it as a protection against the effect of global inflation, as an instrument for financing education in the life of his children - so that a righteous man continues to leave an inheritance for his children's children, which includes educational inheritance.

Finance in the life of the believer helps in the pursuit of one's personal projects and in the carrying out and executing of capital projects.

When a believer experiences the great wealth transfer they are able to give their children a head start in life so the instruments God will use will be education. However for the believer also, a great wealth transfer can help the management of the later life through pension schemes and retirement.

# THE STRATEGIES FOR THE WEALTH TRANSFER

The great wealth transfer would require two keys to combine in order for that transfer to be effected. It is like walking into your bank and requesting that funds be transferred to another account or nation. Most banks have a procedure which will be considered to have been completed before such a transaction can be effected.

The great wealth transfer would require combining the

prophecy with principles. These principles will primarily include the strategy for making the wealth available. Jesus does not only believe in us holding onto the prophecy, He expects us to apply the principles.

He once told the parable of the talents, a story which had a lot to do with investment since a talent in Bible times was more like a gold bar and someone had said each talent was worth about $547,000. In the story Jesus told, the man who was given two talents doubled it and the one given five did the same. However, the man who was given one talent buried it. Judging by the action of the man who was given one talent, it was possible that if he had a role reversal with the man who was given five talents he would have done the same thing, buried the talents. After all his excuse for not multiplying the talent was not the size. He had an attitude problem. There are certain principles which need to be in place and applied for the wealth transfer to be effected.

In this chapter we will take these principles one by one.

## 1. Creativity

*But remember the LORD your God for it is he who gives you the ability to produce wealth and so confirms his covenant which he swore to your forefathers as it is today. Deuteronomy 8:18*

In this verse, the words 'ability to produce wealth' also means to create wealth. Creativity involves work. Work that shows the creative skill of the individual. Work that solves the problems which people face. You cannot know wealth until you solve problems for people.

Creativity is like a far fetched way to create wealth. However, it is basically bringing solutions to problems. Therefore wherever there are problems there are opportunities, and where there are opportunities creativity has found a birthplace. More problems, more opportunities, more creativity.

Being creative means not just talking about issues but thinking solution. Many of today's wealthy people in the secular world are creative in the things we do regularly and ordinarily. The comedian, Bill Cosby became a multi-millionaire by telling funny jokes. The wealthiest black woman on earth, Oprah Winfrey became worth $1.2 billion through talking.

Many have found that their creativity is in things like growing food, cooking it, public relations or boxing. If it isn't creative and imaginative just to think that a man is being paid to fight! Whatever it is, it is a matter of having the capacity to see yourself turning a passion into a channel for expressing creativity.

> "If you see yourself as prosperous, you will be. If you see yourself as continually hard up, that is exactly what you will be." - **Robert Collier**

## 2. Innovation

This is the ability to think out of the box. In other words, a deviation from what is the regular and acceptable. The modern man has no problem with innovation because much of what we call advanced technology today was as a result of thinking outside of the box. It is as a result of making up one's mind to create cutting edge technology.

Every time a new thing shows up in the market, it changes how everybody thinks, it causes an adjustment, an about turn. Many times people will refer to you and rebuke you for trying to be different, yet they would often pay for anything that gives a feeling of difference.

Prior to the innovative appearance of the personal computer, all that was known of computers were large mainframes which occupied whole rooms. Then came IBM with innovative thinking, creating computers which are personal and usable and could be placed on desktop. Since then, the rest has been history.

The opposite of innovation is conformity, custom, habit, tradition, consistency, regularity and sameness.

> "Wealth is in application of mind to nature; and the art of getting rich consists not in industry, much less in saving, but in a better order, in timeliness, in being at the right spot." - **Ralph Waldo Emerson**

## 3. Space

This is doing business with the ability to play on a larger field. The scriptures talk about the work of your hands, your basket and your field.

*Your basket and your kneading trough will be blessed.*
*Deuteronomy 28:5*

*The LORD will send a blessing on your barns and on everything you put your hand to. The LORD your God will bless you in the land he is giving you. Deuteronomy 28:8*

*The LORD will grant you abundant prosperity-in the fruit of your womb, the young of your livestock and the crops of your ground-in the land he swore to your forefathers to give you. The LORD will open the heavens, the storehouse of his bounty, to send rain on your land in season and to bless all the work of your hands. You will lend to many nations but will borrow from none. Deuteronomy 28:11-12*

The space created by the works of your hand is no bigger than your pocket. Therefore you are limited by space. The work of your hand kind of business possibly has no employees. Level two is your basket. It is a small to medium scale enterprise hiring a handful of staff to cover basic necessities. But the third level, the storehouse kind of business is in larger space, not only in the magnitude of operation but in the project management method which allows for capacity building.

When your space is small, mental, financial, physical, structural chaos and problems are inevitable and possibly continuous. However, the bigger the space for your business the greater your manoeuvre.

This leads us to the fourth point.

## 4. Manoeuvrability

By this we mean your ability to move or to create movement, your wisdom and strength to manipulate a difficult situation until it begins to produce positive results. It is very difficult to go very far in business and create great wealth if you do not know how to navigate within the business world.

You are constantly surrounded by business sharks who would take advantage at any sign of immaturity or inability. To be able to manoeuvre includes the ability to negotiate, to handle the opposition and to persevere when things are difficult.

To manoeuvre would require the ability to exercise patience until the business bears fruits. When a spirit-filled Christian combines his sense of spiritual discernment with the ability to manoeuvre he is able to pick out those who are doing business with underhandedness, trickery or wiles.

## 5. Connection

This is the ability to network for greater effect. It is impossible to clap with one hand. The reason for publicly floated businesses is in order to spread the risk and allow others to participate. All publicly floated companies create the opportunity for others to hold shares and therefore put their money down to make their business go forward.

As God prepares believers to receive the wealth He will transfer, there has to be a transformation of mind and the recognition that we only become bigger and stronger through unity.

*How good and pleasant it is when brothers live together in unity!*
*Psalm 133:1*

## 6. Be informed

This is not a mere gathering of information but creating the atmosphere where you are an authority on one thing, narrowing down information on one matter until you know so much about it. Building your dreams, ideas and vision around one thing which God can use to transfer wealth to you.

This may require building your day and relationships around it. It might require studying the top ten people around that particular subject: what they did to get to the top, how they have managed to stay at the top, what they continue to do to keep increasing.

If you must turn that idea to your source of wealth you cannot be ashamed of it and you must always want to discuss it with practically everyone you meet. You must ensure that it is solving a problem and know very well what problem it solves.

Do research on who will benefit from that product so it helps you know who you are marketing it to and the likely financial and physical benefits from it.

## 7. Assemble a team

*How could one man chase a thousand or two put ten thousand to flight unless their Rock had sold them unless the LORD had given them up? Deuteronomy 32:30*

You cannot have the spirit and approach of a lone ranger if you intend to experience a major wealth transfer. You will need to assemble a team, a group of people who believe and share your dreams and ideas or at least workers who are not only there to solve a money problem for themselves but who are excited to see results follow whatever they do with you or for you.

This team must be motivated and the chief motivating officer will have to be YOU. After all, it is your dream they came to make happen.

*All these were fighting men who volunteered to serve in the ranks. They came to Hebron fully determined to make David king over all Israel. All the rest of the Israelites were also of one mind to make David king. 1 Chronicles 12:38*

Define their reward. Every human being on earth is motivated by a rewarding system. You have got to know the way to a man's heart and therefore create a system which adequately rewards them. Show them what to achieve if this reward must come into their hand. Give people a reason for participating in your vision. Let them see why they should be excited in making your dream happen.

Supervise those who are linked up to your vision. Never totally leave your vision in the hands of a team without being the chief motivator. No one fully understands your vision like you do and therefore the constant motivation must come from you.

## 8. Be order conscious

*But everything should be done in a fitting and orderly way.
1 Corinthians 14:40*

Order creates comfort in anything you do. Financial problems and family challenges are often products of disorder. If finances are not running well, disorder has been created somewhere. Sickness is a result of disorder in the physical body.

All poor nations have one thing in common, they are very disorderly. Disorder manifests when you try to do what you are not created to do. Disorder occurs when you abandon the priorities of your life. Disorder will come if you refuse to become whom God ordained you to be. Disorder will happen when you place responsibility on those unprepared or untrained to accept it.

Your weakness grows in the midst of your disorder. People will also take advantage of you once they see that your business life is disorderly. It is easier to pilfer in a company that has no order or a good management process in place. On the other hand, where there is order you have locked the door against strife, wastage and you release a greater degree of comfort.

God is a God of order. He only does things in the sequence of time. The rain has to fall before the seed can germinate. If you look at your life carefully, the areas where you have produced extra are the areas where you have maintained order. So the more order you permit in your life the easier it is to detect disorder and to strengthen your own future.

Become result oriented and truly have the capacity to have and manage great wealth

## 9. Record-keeping

Just as we have previously talked about order, small businesses do not know how to create paper trails. They make decisions and do their accounts on the back of notebooks or small pieces of paper.

It is impossible to be given major things to manage if you are not a good steward of that which was. He has tested you in the days of small beginnings. You cannot dip your hand in the till and help yourself because it is your business. If you want to manage things that are big you have to know how to create a system of personal accountability so that the capital is separated from profits.

In order to operate on this level you might have to move some people away from your circle, who only belong in yesterday, who are not moving towards the creation of order; people who particularly prefer the way you have operated, trying to capture an ocean in a tea cup.

## 10. Market your product

Primarily you must learn to place your products where the people are, therefore giving it the best access. It is no use writing a book when you have no market. Because you are passionate about it does not mean everyone is. It is no use designing clothes if no one wants them. Because you are passionate about it does not mean everybody is.

If your product has not sold, it is either that people do not want it or that you have not properly placed it before them.

## 11. Know what people want

In my travel I often meet believers who fall in love with their own little ideas, unknown to them that if you want to test an idea, you do not submit it only to a friend but also to a mentor who will truly subject it to a lot of testing and be honest with you.

Knowing what people require and want, you must consider:

### a. The quality of the product

Is it of the highest you can produce or the highest standard in the market? Because the quality of your product already determines the level at which it enters into the market.

### b. Is it easy to use?

Some people give simple things a complicated approach thus making everyone turn away from it; while there are certain people who are skilful in taking the most complicated things and breaking them down in concrete form for those who do not think in abstract terms.

### c. Ensure people are getting value for their money

Let people always feel that they are getting a bargain. If a product is expensive and yet you have a method for making people feel that they are getting a bargain, people will be ready to part with money. After all, it conveys a sense of value to them.

**K I S S** - **K**eep **I**t **S**imple **S**ugar. This is an expression to say, whatever you do and whatever way you present your products, if there is to be a wealth transfer you must know how to make it simple even if you have to use the services of a consultant who thinks and speaks the language of those who are your end users.

## 12. Create a sense of satisfaction

It would be utter selfishness to only see what profit you would make from selling a product to people. It is very important to think of equal benefit. You derive benefits from the financial wealth transfer and they derive benefits from getting a product that is of great value.

This benefit must convey the feeling that they have not lost their money but rather that they have got more than a bargain for the money they have spent.

## 13. Negotiate

The art of negotiation may determine if you become a candidate for wealth transfer or not. Paul the Apostle was very good with this. He negotiated effectively the return and acceptance of Onesimus to his master. He was a slave who had offended the master and had run away.

Negotiation takes into account the other person's feelings and yet presents to them the win-win situation. In the negotiation, the reputation and integrity you have must be clear and obvious to those with whom you negotiate.

*And Hiram added: Praise be to the LORD the God of Israel who made heaven and earth! He has given King David a wise son endowed with intelligence and discernment who will build a temple for the LORD and a palace for himself. 2 Chronicles 2:12*

When Paul spoke with Philemon he acknowledged the favours which he had bestowed upon Philemon and requested the same to be done to him. Solomon made reference to past favours for king Hiram to his father and requested for the same to be extended to him.

*Solomon sent this message to Hiram king of Tyre: "Send me cedar logs as you did for my father David when you sent him cedar to build a palace to live in. 2 Chronicles 2:3*

When handling matters of negotiation you must yourself be able to walk away without closure and yet have a good sleep. You must know when not to continue. You must also know when you are being put under undue pressure to make a decision that you may later regret.

A good negotiation cannot be complete without you carrying out your own due process and due diligence before you commit finances to the things you want to buy. If you want to buy a property, you need to carry out an independent valuation and not take the valuation of the person who is selling it to you.

## INVESTMENT

### 14. Why invest?

We have grabbed the bull by the horn by going to the subject of investment. We have not dealt with the concept of the savings account because savings are not ways to build wealth, neither are they ways to experience a transfer of wealth.

One of the key reasons why this is obvious is there is no economy right now in the world where maintaining a savings account results in any form of wealth creation. Whatever interest is placed on the finance you leave in a savings account is limited and is often washed away by the nations' annual inflationary figure.

Investment is a wise action because it helps to protect your assets and the things God is providing against the effects of inflation. If you leave $5,000 in an account with an interest rate of three or four per cent while the inflation of the nation is at five to six per cent, even though you potentially have a couple of dollars added to your money as interest, the value of your money has dwindled because the rate of inflation is higher than the interest which has accrued on your money.

In the story of the talents, the man who came back with one talent did not really quite come back with one talent because it was now one talent minus the rate of inflation. He had ended up with one talent which was now less than its original value.

Investing helps to finance projects. It is my conviction that at different times as believers seize the moment and take advantage of investment opportunities i.e. in the stock market or in real estate, as the dividends begin to come, it gives them the opportunity when visions are presented by the field marshals of the Gospel to reach the world, build churches, edifices and touch the community. Such people are able to draw from the finance God has provided.

Not only does investing help to finance the projects of Christian ministries, it helps to finance personal projects so that the dreams and aspirations of the individuals become a reality.

Investment gives you the opportunity to give your children a head start. Imagine yourself running with one of the fastest runners on earth, previous or current - Karl Lewis, Linford Christie of Britain etc. If you were not a trained athlete who could do a 100 metres under ten seconds it would be impossible to keep up with these men.

However imagine if you were put half way down the track, that is 50 metres to the tape of a 100 metre race. Even if you did not finish first, you would not be too far behind any of them. That is what it means to be given a head start.

A good education, accommodation to live in as you leave school or some capital with which to start business certainly is a way to give children a head start. It makes them immediately shoulders high above their mates.

Investing helps you to handle the latter years of life. Imagine your life being broken into three equal parts. Zero to 30 would be the morning of life, 30 to 50 possibly would be the afternoon of life and 50 and above would be the evening.

The early years are learning years. The middle years are earning years while the latter part is the yearning season of life.

It would be unwise to do in the evening what you should have done in the afternoon. In every society, culture, city, town or hamlet you will meet people who are now trying to struggle in the evening of their life to make ends meet, probably because they did not make much investment during their work seasons of life. They did not question their level of income to ensure that they were also able to put something in the future before the future came.

Putting something in the future is more like the interpretation Joseph brought for the dream of the Pharaoh. When Joseph asked them to keep in store for seven years food against the seven lean years, that meant that the better years were to take care of the years that were lean. This is a major reason for investing.

## 15. Concepts of investment

### a. Securities or financial assets

This could be documents indicating ownership or creditorship or a stock certificate. Securities are assets, revenue reserves tied up in a way that gives the owner the peace of mind that it cannot be easily taken or stolen.

### b. Returns

Returns are the things that accrue to a person after they have made investments. It is the profit or interest yielded from a labour investment or expenditure.

### c. Risk

This is the danger or probability of loss or gain when you invest in any endeavour. Investments do have risks. It is the exposure or the chance of a loss or damage which you are likely to face. The reason many people never build wealth therefore is that the aspect of risk becomes a concern to them so they put their money in savings accounts and whereas life is a risk in itself.

If you are sitting down to read this book or listen to it on tape, you have taken a risk because the chair could have broken down. If you are in a multi-storey building, there could have been an architectural fault.

Life is riskier without first the probability of losing money that the higher the risk the higher the returns. Every investment that brings a higher return tends to have a higher risk.

## d. Diversification.

This is the concept of spreading your finance on various kinds of investments so that you are not a 100 per cent focused on one method of investments, i.e. stocks and shares or just real estate.

It might also be viewed as a way to create a multiple stream of income because streams are in various sizes. One stream may be constant while the other brings only trickles. However the ones which bring trickles may be more assuring than those which bring large returns but only once in a while.

## e. Compounded interest

When investment earnings are added to the principal forming a larger base on which earnings may accumulate, it is called compounding. In other words, if you make profit and you don't spend the profit but rather reinvest it and the original capital, you have now compounded your interest. The more you do this the more you keep compounding the interest that accrues to you.

## 16. Understand the investment environment

God created the environment for Israel to be able to spoil the Egyptians and take all their gold. That was an atmosphere of supernatural favour. Every nation has its atmosphere for investment and wealth creation. Some have greater opportunities than others.

If you are investing in the British stock market, your rates of return may be very low however, it is stable and almost predictable except when a major catastrophe happens - like the crash of the technology shares.

This is completely opposite to investing in a third world situation like Ghana, which also has a degree of stability. However, the number of people involved in the stock and shares market of Ghana, compared to the population, are limited. Therefore the rate of return for those who participate is very high.

If on the other hand your investment requires borrowing money, borrowing in a country like Britain where interest rates are low gives you an advantage over a place like Ghana. The reason is that larger and stronger economies tend to have a lower cost on the capital available for investment. Their inflation is also lower because the economy is more robust.

A third world nation like Ghana will pose a greater challenge if you want to do international business and have to exchange your local currency. You will need a lot of it to be able to exchange on the international market into a foreign currency with which you need to carry out your transactions.

Therefore, an understanding of the environment in which you do your business must be clear to you before you venture.

## 17. Investment opportunities

If you must be the person to whom God will transfer the coming great wealth to, you must learn to allow your eyes to be opened to see the investment opportunities that will cause this inflow of supernatural finance.

There are several ways this could happen, however, let us quickly look at five.

### a. Involvement in the goods industry

Remember God will always want to put His blessing on something. He said He would bless your basket or your storehouse. Involvement in the goods industry means producing for a market.

This, of course, will have to be something people need and are ready to exchange their money for.

### b. Involvement in the service industry

The richest man for a couple of years running is still William Gates. The source of his wealth has not been the production of goods per se, but the production of a service. His Windows software practically runs PCs all over the world.

While seated behind your computer somewhere in Africa and on the internet you could download software from Microsoft for a fee, using your credit card to pay.

One of the reasons why third world nations continue to remain poor is because the industrial nations that were essentially their colonial masters moved from the emphasis of being a goods society to a service oriented society. But third world nations have not moved.

## c. Involvement in real estate

All through the Bible and even in our modern times, the fastest, greatest and best way for a wealth shift has always been real estate. You do not need expertise beyond the regular to manage real estate.

If you buy in the right city, returns can be fast and unlike stocks and shares, buying in the right neighbourhood would mean that somebody else's property can pull yours up in value. Stocks and shares don't do that.

## d. Involvement in financial securities

The money market has various options for investment even though they may be limited in their returns. Fixed deposits, certificates of deposits, bonds, treasury bills etc.

## e. Involvement in collective investment

Unit trusts, savings and loans. A unit trust is "a financial product where money from a number of investors is pulled together and invested collectively in investments such as shares and bonds. Each investor owns a unit (or a number of them) the value of which depends on the value of those items owned by the fund. A unit trust allows modest investment to be diversified away from a holding in a single or small number of companies."[1]

The unit trust is further defined as an open ended collective investment fund divided into units, each representing an identical fraction of the total underlying investment. The investment fund is set up under a trust deed. The investor is effectively the beneficiary under the trust.

The beauty of a unit trust or savings and loan deposit is that it takes the power of many people to create a pool of funds with which to continue to do business so that everyone in the end is supposed to win.

On the other hand, a savings and loan association is a financial institution which specialises in accepting savings, deposits and making mortgage loans.

They are often mutually held, meaning that the depositors and borrowers are members with voting rights and have the ability to direct the financial and managerial goals of the organisation. It is possible for a savings and loan association to be stock based and even publicly traded.[2]

## 18. Finding your investments

You cannot draw from where you have not made a deposit. Again, back to the story of the talent. The man

[1] www.mliminternational.com/xxcite/individual-investors/glossary2html
[2] www.wikkipedia.org/wikki/savingsandloans

who buried the one talent was foolish in his action but wise in a statement he made.

He said to his boss, "You want to draw where you have not made a deposit."

This book challenges us to recognise the seasons for a great wealth transfer. However, every one of God's miracles require a previous action. You must be able to show your capacity to release what is in your hand in order for you to come into the blessing God has for you.

You must increase disposable income. In other words, increase how much you put in your investment and decrease how much you take out. The pain of many businesses is when those who invest in it quickly begin to draw a little profit which accrues but gratification would need to be delayed so that as you learn to delay your gratification you are able to compound the profit.

Delayed gratification is a sign of maturity. Delayed gratification will require that you embrace a saving and investment culture and a deliberate act of walking in need, not because you did not have the funds with which to make the supply but because you want to compound the interest on what you have.

Your spending could also be controlled. This could be done by making up your mind on how you intend to manage your income. You could do the 10-10-80 principle. Ten per cent is the tithe that goes to God. Ten per cent goes into a personal savings account and the remaining eighty per cent is used in various investments and the meeting of your personal needs.

## 19. Have an approach towards wealth creation

This must start with a definition of your objectives. Why exactly are you setting out to create wealth? Some of this we have already dealt with earlier on. But the primary challenge before the believer is to create wealth in order to advance the Gospel, making himself a candidate for the great transfer of wealth which God is about to bring to pass.

However, not just that, enjoying some of the dividends of the wealth created by using it to bless your generation, your children and creating a level of comfort for yourself. You must answer certain questions:

- Why am I investing?

- What am I investing?

- When will I invest?

- How do I want to invest - real estate, stocks, unit trusts, goods industry?

Choose an investment advisor. Solomon said that "By wisdom you should make war."

*Wisdom is better than weapons of war but one sinner destroys much good. Ecclesiastes 9:18*

Creating wealth requires a certain skill, particularly if it is an area where you have not been involved in the past. Therefore conducting research becomes necessary, however, that in itself is not enough. You need experts who will give you counsel.

With the counsel given, you must study your playing field, the nation in which you are investing and marry your objective with the realities on the ground so that you can maximise your realities with your objectives. Once this is clarified it is time to take action.

## 20. Master strategies for wealth creation

Do not forget that this book is premised on the fact that it is only God who gives the increase.

*I planted the seed, Apollos watered it, but God made it grow.*
*1 Corinthians 3:6*

With that in mind, there are areas which have been proven to be great sources of financial multiplication. Let me present some of these to you:

## a. Real estate

The use of real estate or home ownership to build wealth is in my opinion one of the greatest methods for increase. Remember the earth is the Lord's and the fullness thereof and He has given us everything richly to enjoy.

The beauty of real estate is that even if you make mistakes in the purchase of land and houses, you can easily recover because part of the mistakes could be buying without equity - that is if a building were worth $50,000 and you ended up buying it for $50,000 that is at a zero equity. And if property prices do not increase on time in the area, your money does not produce wealth.

However if you have chosen the city, town or place carefully and bought, you can recover from mistakes. You can work with other people's money also. Banks are always interested to give loans to buy properties. No bank will ever give you money to buy stocks and shares. With properties, value can increase with minimal investment.

Several people who sell houses or properties do not know that with a little painting here and there, with a little changing of a few broken things, the value can be raised by a higher percentage. Were you to use a mortgage to buy that would have been a smart action.

A mortgage is using other people's money as principal payment for the building; so you use other people's money to buy other people's houses. If it was buy-to-let you would also be using other people's money to pay the rent, as such persons occupy the building.

When you invest in real estate, unlike the stock exchange, you do not need to monitor how a property is doing on a minute by minute basis. Every payment you make towards reducing the money borrowed and the interest it accrues means that you are increasing the equity on the house.

Dictionary.com defines equity as "The residual value of a business or property beyond any mortgage thereon and liability therein." This could also be attributed to the money you invested in anything, however, as it relates to property it is more or less what would be handed to you were you to return the mortgage borrowed to the borrowers.

It goes without saying that real great wealth can be built through real estate. It is not easily dated while a lot of stock and shares are. The danger would be to buy out of emotional attachment. I have known people who have gone to buy real estate or a building in their hometown when really, properties do not perform well in the town of their birth.

The key thing is to study your nation and know where property does well. Most times, it is either the capital or the business city of a nation. This is because people are always drawn to these cities, therefore needing accommodation.

Where it is not houses to live in, even commercial properties will only carry value if they are in the business cities of the land. Most wealthy people keep their wealth in real estate.

## b. Investment in overseas markets

This book is written with the intention to challenge believers to prepare themselves for a wealth transfer. It is going to be on a global level. It is beyond what people do at their local stations.

You may not be able to go everywhere and participate in every form of business venture, however, there are stocks, shares and mutual funds that are globally placed. The internet has made the world a global village. You can access this information and where you are not savvy enough, it would be wise to use the services of an expert, particularly one who knows much about global investment.

## c. Use other people's money

It is very important for you to know the need for creating leverage in order to really break through in business. If you operate as an individual, there is a limit to the funds available to you.

In the scriptures we are told that the prophet told the woman to go and borrow vessels and not to borrow a few. Leveraging means using what other people have in order to increase your capacity.

The church is in constant debate as to whether Christians should borrow. Those who hold the view that Christians should not borrow are very intense about it. They quote scriptures like, "Owe no man anything but love."

However that leaves Christian business in danger because they have not diluted their risk, neither have they taken advantage of funds that could be available for them to be able to facilitate and play on a bigger field.

Sourcing funds by using other people's money has its advantages. Borrowing for upward investment changes the base of your operation. It is actually tapping into the financial risk of other people so you can do extraordinary things.

When Jesus spoke about the talents as we have referred to several times, He was talking about leveraging. These men had nothing and suddenly, talents were handed over to them.

Once you have access to such funds, it is important to learn how to manage the cashflow.

Great wealth will further be created as you learn, not only to manage the cashflow but to improve the various techniques by which you do this.

Recent authors like Robert Kiyosaki have shown that the ability to manage the payables versus the receivables can help to compound funds in your hand.

## d. Conduct market research

This is necessary in order to know what your competitors are doing. Secondly, in order to know what your clients need.

Great enterprises are only built by keeping abreast of facts.

*Any enterprise is built by wise planning, becomes strong through common sense, and profits wonderfully by keeping abreast of the facts. Proverbs 24:3-4 (Living Bible)*

## e. Be committed to excellence

It is necessary to commit yourself to excellence if you must really increase wealth. Mediocrity is very easy. It is not difficult to produce shabby products; however, when you are committed to excellence and you carry it out, you distinguish yourself and create a niche for yourself.

This act of excellence is not easy to create. It takes drive, stamina and determination; however it is what successful people do.

Mediocrity is not hard to know in companies. You could tell that some people are only out to make money, not to make an impact or change society. People can see through a mediocre company; however, the most successful businesses which you know of strive to be greater than their competitors by delivering superior customer service and experience.

So excellence is daring yourself to be better than you were yesterday.

It is doing everything in your power to get where your dreams would take you.

Excellence is creating a strategy by which you will consistently exceed consumer expectation.

It is that by which you will put in place and will end up being able to guarantee yourself that certain customers will stay with you for life.

## f. Creating employment

Part of this great wealth transfer will mean that God is looking for people whom He can use as a distribution centre for His wealth.

*"I will make you into a great nation and I will bless you; I will make your name great and you will be a blessing. Genesis 12:2*

When God told Abraham that he would be a blessing, God intended for him to come into the revelation of a higher level of blessing than that which is personal.

Level one was 'you will be blessed' but level two was 'you will be a blessing, you will distribute to others'.

Part of distribution of the great wealth that shall be transferred is by empowering those who work with you. However, your choice of employees immediately determines the quality of your output and the quantity of your result.

You need to define the corporate culture you want to create before you go out looking for employees. Do not hire cheap or else you will end up with a cheap company.

## g. Create streams of income

There is something interesting about the sea. Whether it is Atlantic or Indian, Mediterranean or Baltic, one thing characterises the sea; it is a large expanse of water. However, it is interesting that rivers and streams, though smaller, empty their water into the sea.

Creating multiple streams of income means that you can be creative enough to make various streams bring water to your sea. One of the challenges of the modern man is the fact that he has created boxes and cultures of work that have ended in entrapment.

We graduate young men and women through universities whose only ambition is to get a job and stay in a structured method of office. Their whole desire is to have their needs met. They have no dreams, no fire in their bones that makes them think beyond that one job. They organise their life around it with only a desire to work in that nine-to-five setting and at the end of their work day, to go for all forms of recreation.

We do not see in scripture anyone whom God transferred wealth to because they had a job. Neither do we see it in today's' world. It is hard for you to meet a nine-to-five man who is a millionaire.

When I say a million, forgive me if I have to use the US dollar as a barometer here for measuring a millionaire. It is no use reading the strategies for wealth creation if your desire and ambition is to stay in a JOB - Just Over Broke.

The strategies we have enumerated in this chapter are not exhaustive. There could be others that God could give you.

The intention here was to stroke your mind for you to begin to see the possibilities, to dream a new dream or catch a new vision.

# DEVELOPING THE MINDSET FOR WEALTH CREATION

The mind is the centre of man's personality. When we get born-again, our spirit immediately, by reason of rebirth becomes a member of the family of God; however, our minds are still influenced by the things we have been through, the way we were raised or the environment in which we live.

That's why Solomon said,

> *For as he thinketh in his heart so is he: Eat and drink*
> *saith he to thee; but his heart is not with thee. Proverbs 23:7*

Our thought life is very powerful. Defeat or victory, blessing or cursing continues depending on the kind of mindset or thought life you have chosen to cultivate.

In this chapter, we want to take a detailed look at how wealthy people think and operate, how they view losses or gain.

Wealthy people have a different mindset from the poor and the middle class. We will later see the three distinctions, however we are saying that your mindset can help or hold you back from a life of wealth.

If the great transfer must take place and if you are to be an active participant, then you must choose to refute the thoughts which do not empower you towards your vision of financial increase.

Wherever you are today is a product of your old way of thinking and acting. Whatever result you have around you is a reflection, not just of your environment but also of your inner thoughts.

It goes without saying therefore that if you must move to a higher level and enter your wealthy place, your old way of thinking will have to be dropped for a new one. The quality of your thoughts and vision must be raised to the level where it can produce and handle the wealth which God is about to transfer to the Body of Christ.

When people meet you or interact with you there are

conclusions they draw based on the wealth of what comes out of your mind. The strength to handle losses, the capacity to think broadly will be dependent on how your mind has been trained.

When wealthy people with the right mindset lose wealth for example, they tend to gain it back because of the kind of habits and thought patterns they have formed. During a slow economic period in Asia, a gentleman who had lost about $4 billion dollars as a result of all his stocks and shares wiped out at such season was seen a couple of days later playing golf. When asked why he didn't lose his mind and why he was playing golf, his remark was that he knew what he did to gain the wealth and he knows what to do to gain it back.

I find that the irony of our planet is that 80 per cent of people never reach their full potential. They never walk in true happiness as a result of using the mind which God has given them to full capacity. A lot of people focus on the fruits of labour rather than the roots and seeds that created the fruit.

The fruit is always visible but the root is not. However it is that which is invisible which results in the visible. If you therefore want to change the fruit you would have to change the root. If a man is not pleased with his financial results, until he changes the root which produces the fruit, he remains perpetually unhappy.

To change this fruit you may have to strengthen the root in order to change the quality of the fruit that hangs on your financial tree. So many people do not realise that in upbringing, the thoughts sown into their mind by parents, friends, etc. have already set the root of their financial life.

Whatever is around you is a result. Wealth is a result, money is a result. Health or illness are all results. Your inner thoughts create your outer world. The man who was given one talent certainly had roots that could not produce abundant fruits so if he had been given the five talents it would have still remained dumped. He would probably not have been able to handle it.

The inner convictions of the man with one talent created his outer world. His attitude to finance and wealth were formed and programmed either as a child or in the environment of his upbringing. He was not born with it.

No one was born with an attitude towards finance. We were taught rightly or wrongly. What you know about finance was modelled by programming and by specific incidents in your family.

How is this programming done? No one ever sits you down to say, "I am going to teach you how to remain poor or being able to manage finance." No one ever says, "I am going to teach you to only be able to micro-manage finance and not be able to handle large volumes of wealth."

Whatever is done to us is always that people keep making statements like "Not everyone can be rich. There is never enough in the world. We could never afford it. Money does not buy happiness. You cannot be rich and spiritual. You have to work hard to make money. Money does not grow on trees or, you cannot be rich."

Some have gone as far as saying, "Rich people are greedy, or, save your money for a rainy day etc."

Whatever you allow to sift through into the premise of your spirit, into the crevices of your heart will determine your thinking. Your daily thinking will end up influencing your decisions. Your decision-making pattern will predict your actions and your actions will set your outcome.

In a nutshell, whatever is at the root of your desire or anger at wealth would fix the result you have. If you are an angry person or full of fear, all you will be doing is expressing that exact emotion and therefore create barriers to becoming the candidates to be used of God in wealth creation.

## YOUR MONEY BLUEPRINT

Every house started as a blueprint before it was erected. No bricklayer or structural engineer will go outside of what the architect has designed. The purpose of a blueprint is in order to give shape and pattern to a building. While the blueprint is designed, the shape of things to come is already fixed.

If the house stands for long or not is already determined. If you want to know what kind of money blueprint you have had in your life, in order to understand the concept of money blueprint and its impact, you need to take a look at your financial results, your bank account, income, net worth, investments, business success and your spending or saving culture.

The concept of money blueprint is very powerful. It is

the reason for many relationship or marital breakups, possibly because if two people with a mismatch of a blueprint come together, it will be very hard for them to understand each other financially.

Imagine a house designed to be round being built on a foundation that is square - it will not fit.

Your money blueprint determines if money flows to you or if it flows away. Your financial life can be like a river - you are always standing at one point where the river is flowing to or where it is flowing from. For many people their financial river is always flowing away, not to them.

This concept of money blueprint is another way to present the argument about how your thoughts influence your income. Every thought you have is either an investment or an expense. Your thoughts are either blessing you or cursing you.

You can choose to think and act like wealthy people do and that way create the result which you desire and which they create. However, you can choose to think and act contrary. Any which way you do it, the human mind is like a filing cabinet. If the information inside does not support financial success your life will not go in that direction.

The first way to therefore begin to change in order to experience financial wealth is to change the way people think. Some think life just happens unknown to them that they are part of the creation of their own life, success or mediocrity.

When others do not show things have really gone the way they want, they have a habit of blaming the economy, the government, the stock market, the stock brokers, the tax on business, the employer, the employees, the manager, the head office, God etc.

This is not the best approach to solving a mindset problem. There is also another group who choose to hang around complainers. These complainers who put on a victimitis attitude do not recognise that you are part of the creation of wealth or non-wealth or the in-betweens in your life.

## THE POOR MINDSET

Once the concrete of the mind has been set in our attitude towards finance, it takes a toll as it affects the way we view life, how we react to every news that come on radio, television, etc.

Imagine two people watching the news about the hurricane Katrina which blew apart the city of New Orleans. A man with a wealthy mindset will first of all see the magnitude of the challenges it has created for the people of the city. Then he will see the chance to make a contribution in rebuilding the city and then thirdly, the chance to be able to use his business.

A poor person will only see the hurricane, blame God and blame the government for not building enough protection. Poor people play the money game in order not to lose. They are very risk averse. They prefer to be comfortable with the little they do with money but those who believe and must get ready for a great wealth transfer are those who have developed their mind to handle wealth and they tend to end up that way.

Poor people have a desire to experience wealth but their mindset stops them. You cannot experience real wealth if your attitude is that of excuses. The mindset of the poor man makes him give excuses like, "What if I make it and lose it? What if I experience high tax? It is too much work, I could lose my health trying! Everyone is going to want a handout one day if I get wealthy! I could give up! My kids could be kidnapped! It is too much responsibility to handle great wealth! What if I make it and lose it? I will never know if people like me for myself or for my money.

This mindset in itself is a barrier to the poor man and therefore, his money fears work against him.

The poor man's mindset also makes him unsure about what exactly he wants. The greatest reason why many people never get what they desire is that they do not really know what they desire.

There are three attitudes when it comes to the breakthrough of wealth - those who want it, those who choose it and those who are committed to experiencing it.

You must be committed for you to experience the great wealth transfer. If you are not fully and totally committed to wealth creation, the chances are that you will never.

## CONFLICTING WORLD VIEWS

Another major result of the mindset is the creation of

world views. All human beings are essentially influenced by their world view. It is this world view which therefore influences and affects us. It determines if we will be able to handle wealth or not. It is also that world view that will determine what we do when the wealth comes.

The greatest purpose of life is to add value to others and the generations to come. If you have a godly world view and God puts wealth in your hand it goes without saying that your purpose for that wealth will therefore be to carry out world evangelism, help build churches and touch humanity. After all Jesus said, when you give a cup of water to one, "We gave it to Him."

*"Then the righteous will answer him, 'Lord, when did we see you hungry and feed you, or thirsty and give you something to drink? When did we see you a stranger and invite you in, or needing clothes and clothe you? When did we see you sick or in prison and go to visit you?' "The King will reply, 'I tell you the truth, whatever you did for one of the least of these brothers of mine, you did for me.' Matthew 25:37-40*

A godly world view will help you to truly add value and make you come into continuous blessing and rewards from God. True prosperity is a result of sharing your gift and valuables with people who need it.

The conflicting world view here though is that of the poor and the wealthy. They look at the world and life from the window of where they are. We gave an illustration of hurricane Katrina earlier. Whenever there is a disaster, a chaotic problem or a challenge anywhere, the wealthy see opportunities, the poor see obstacles.

The wealthy see potential growth, the poor see potential loss. The wealthy focus on the rewards, even in the most difficult situations, the poor focus on the risks involved. Wealth people take responsibility and make up their mind that with God, they can do valiantly and make things work.

*Through God we will do valiantly for it is He who shall tread down our enemies. Psalm 60:12*

Wealthy people expect to succeed.

*The hope of the righteous shall be gladness: but the expectation of the wicked shall perish. Proverbs 10:28*

They are always willing to take risks and believe that even if it goes wrong, they can always come back. On the other hand, poor people stall whenever they have an opportunity. They call it, "waiting for that opportunity."

The mindset that is ready to handle the wealth that shall be transferred often focuses on what can and will be achieved, while the focus of the poor is on what they do not want. The interesting thing about focusing is that what you focus on expands, what you focus on becomes your experience.

Wealthy people always get started. They take actions, while poor people do not trust themselves or their own abilities. They believe they must know enough and that everything is impossible.

These conflicting perspectives are also expressed by way of their encounters with successful people. The poor and the wealthy react differently at the appearance of success or successful people.

When a wealthy person sees a successful person or project, they celebrate it, embrace it and want to view more while the poor resents success, particularly when they see it in others.

This might not be the action of every poor person but in general, this truth is captured in the words of the Christian author, Russell H Conwell, in his book 'Acres of Diamond.' He said, "We preach against covetousness, and you know we do, in the pulpit, and oftentimes preach against it so long and use the terms about "filthy lucre" so extremely that Christians get the idea that when we stand in the pulpit we believe it is wicked for any man to have money…Money is power, and you ought to be reasonably ambitious to have it! You ought because you can do more good with it than you could without it. Money printed your Bible, money builds your churches, money sends your missionaries…I say then, you ought to have money."[3]

What you resent never increases for you. What you celebrate flows in your direction. Resenting those who are blessed is probably one way to stay broke. We are not permitted to get involved in any form of the deification of money, however it is biblical and Christian to admire, bless and love other blessed people. It is our indirect way to be one of them.

*Rejoice with those who rejoice; mourn with those who mourn.*
*Romans 12:15*

[3]Russell H. Conwell, Acres of Diamonds (Old Tappan, New Jersey: Fleming H. Revell Company, 1960), 20-24

The wealthy choose their association. They do not in any way resent or look down at poor people. However, they choose to associate with those who are positive, successful or in the words of my friend, Robb Thompson, "Those who have empires in their mind."

On the other hand, poor people tend to associate with negative and unsuccessful people. Unlike the wealthy, poor people hear of other people's success and instead of celebrating, they judge, criticise, mock and try to put the successful down.

When a wealthy person hears of another person who is doing well, they build bridges to them, wanting to learn from them. The poor end up with an attitude towards such people. They prefer the group of those who are going nowhere.

You must realise that you cannot hang out with ducks and expect to soar with the eagles.

Wealthy people are prepared to talk about the goodness of God and promote what God has done for them. They look for good Christian causes to promote.

Poor people think negatively about such ideas. Please take note that poverty is not only a money problem, it is also a mind problem. A person could have a good attitude and want to see the Gospel preached and yet does not realise that their actions do not help in the promotion of the Gospel.

There is a great wealth transfer coming; however, it will knock on every door, particularly of believers because God wants to use us to reach the world, preaching the

Gospel of the Kingdom. However, the world view of the poor does not help him.

Wealthy people are usually leaders. They know how to promote what they are doing. This makes them continue to compound and increase the wealth in their hands. When problems arise the wealthy do not go down with it. They feel that they and God are bigger than the problem.

Poor people are smaller than their problems. They accept defeat easily. To be wealthy and stay wealthy would mean having to face challenges, detours, obstacles and roads that are full of traps and pitfalls yet, the wealthy never quit while the poor never wants any hassles, headaches and responsibility. They sure do not want any problems. They just prefer to be in a little corner and have enough to survive.

Success does not come in running away from problems but in taking responsibility, stay until you outgrow the problem. As a matter of fact, the size of the problem you face determines the magnitude of your reward.

It is in this attitude towards problem that the poor and the wealthy tend to define and distinguish themselves.

If you want to be truly successful and wealthy you cannot keep your focus on the size of your problem, rather you should focus on the size you are through God.

*I can do everything through him who gives me strength.*
*Philippians 4:13*

*No, in all these things we are more than conquerors through him who loved us. Romans 8:37*

Your mind is a container. In 2 Kings 4: 1-7 the Prophet of God asked the woman who faced the danger of bankruptcy following the death of her husband, if she had anything in her house; her answer was of course that she had nothing, but a bottle of oil.

The response of Elisha was that she should go and borrow vessels, containers which she would pour the oil into, because the kind of container she had would determine the kind of wealth she could handle.

One of the greatest challenges for many believers is that we are trying to handle a sea in a teacup. We want a wealth transfer, but our mindset has turned out to become a small container; we do not think in large volumes, we do not think of great conquests for God.

God is not a waster of resources. He will not take the wealth of the wicked, who have worked diligently and have achieved great things and put in the hand of a Christian who is unable to balance a couple of dollars, a Christian who is afraid of anything in excess of six figures.

In order to be truly wealthy in God you must consider yourself to be a container. If your container is small, the wealth that comes will be too much and therefore spill over and waste. However, if your container is big you will be able to hold more and use more for the glory of God.

The great wealth transfer coming is going to be much more than the church has ever seen. As I write this book in 2006, I have been a Christian 34 years. When I first became a Christian the church never spoke in millions. Today, across the world even in third world settings, the church has seen a season of harvest.

However the feeling I have is that following the losses that brought us into this new millennium in the economic world, now in 2006 we are in the spring of economic change, the flowers are budding again and there is new life about to hit the finances of the church. God is getting some people ready who He will transfer it into their hands. If this will be you the container must change, you must provide containers for bringing solutions to the challenges of the world. You must find answers to challenges and problems. You need to create systems that handle people's problems because breakthrough essentially is finding problems and solving them. The poor and the successful are always problem oriented, while the successful are always solving them.

Wealthy people are great receivers, poor people are poor receivers. The poor never feel qualified for any blessing in spite of the scriptures they read and as a matter of fact, if your quality of mind is not transformed you will always be looking for scriptures, statements and preachers who justify your present condition.

*Do not conform any longer to the pattern of this world but be transformed by the renewing of your mind. Then you will be able to test and approve what God's will is-his good pleasing and perfect will. Romans 12:2*

The wealthy work hard and they believe it is perfectly appropriate to be rewarded for the effort and the value they provide. The poor have a mindset that says "Money will change me, I might get greedy therefore I am okay as

I am." Either way you will live what you believe.

If you say you are not worthy, then you truly are not. Money will only make you what you already are because money is neutral. Money never changes, it only takes the character of the owner.

Imagine a $100 bill leaving the hand of a banker and getting into the hands of a baker. The baker is a businessman and the first thing he thinks of is how to multiply it. If that same paper ended up in the hand of a drug user, that money immediately takes on the character of the drug addict; it becomes drug money. If it leaves his hand and falls into the hand of a person that a person who brings it to church, it is not drug money, it immediately takes on the character of the believer who loves the Lord and wants to worship God with it, it becomes money used for evangelism. Money therefore is neutral.

## SHIFT THE GEAR OF YOUR MIND

The attitude of the wealthy and the poor on making money is better reflected on how they expect to be paid. The wealthy person chooses to get paid based on result but poor people choose to get paid based on time. The poor person looks at the number of hours and how much you will pay him per hour. There is nothing wrong with such pay cheque, but the only problem is it interferes with you earning what you are truly worth.

Wealthy people usually run their own business therefore making their money from profits. They prefer to work on commission or percentage and make more money through investments. They are usually very time conscious and will not spend all of their life on what should take a shorter time.

Wealthy people believe in themselves and place great value on their ability to deliver while the poor are usually opposite that. The poor will be ready to accept a ceiling placed on their salary because it is tied to their qualification or physical skill. Wealthy people never place a ceiling on their income. They are convinced they live in a world of abundance. Therefore this is the perspective of the world they hold. The poor live in and see a world of limitations. Not enough this or that.

Wealthy people focus on their net worth. Poor people focus on their working income. Wealthy people take the time to keep learning about investments and investing. They go to seminars, read books, watch programs on television that increase their wealth while the poor will prefer the programs that belittle the wealth and undermine their wealth.

Poor people think investing is only for wealthy people. They never make an attempt to learn. When the wealthy and the poor buy newspapers, they turn to different pages. The wealthy turn to the pages that give the current results of the stocks and the shares while poor people will rather look for what they consider either as news or the latest gossip.

Wealthy people manage their money well while poor people mismanage their income and are always waiting for the month to end. If there is going to be a great wealth transfer, the man who cannot manage great wealth, who can only think in terms of a fixed income will not be able to handle the thought of money compounding and also will not be able to release a large sum that he has not personally conquered. He is unable to release that sum of money to be used for the work of ministry. That way, he disqualifies himself to be a candidate of the great wealth transfer.

If a person does not manage money well it was because he was never programmed to do so. After all, money management is not a course in any school; however it is a habit we learn. The habit of money management is more important than the amount to be managed because the person who has developed the habit of investing will increase whatever is given to them, even if it is little.

Imagine the man who was given two talents. If he were the one given one talent, by the time the master came it would have become two talents. The man who was given one talent on the other hand, were he the one given two, it would have remained the same number.

Until you show that you can handle more it is impossible for you to have it. Once in a while somebody with a poor mindset has stumbled on some money, either through ungodly ways i.e. lottery, gambling or stealing; the interesting thing is they don't control the money, it ends up controlling them.

Work, work, work. The mindset determines how the poor and the wealthy view working. The poor think working hard is what produces, while the wealthy believe in working smart.

Wealthy people have their money working hard for them through investments after they have worked for it. While the wealthy man is in bed, his money put into various investments is working for him. Poor people on the other hand work hard and never make enough money.
Wealthy people make their money work for them through treasury bonds, stocks, mutual funds, mortgages, real estate, royalties, on box, music, software and any intellectual property they have, licensing, owning of vending businesses etc.

They think long term, not barely making ends meet and making sure they survive. Most of the financial plans of a poor person is short term; how to go from one month end to the other. If anything distinguishes the poor and the wealthy, it is their spending habits.

The wealthy tend to have a lot of money but form a habit of spending little while poor people have a little money but are into spending a lot.

Here in 2006, as I sat down to write this book I went on the internet and I was surprised to see that the wealthiest man in the world, worth $48 billion dollars, Bill Gates still drives a car that is seven years old, a 1999 Porsche. It is not for want of enough money to buy a new one. In fact, I think he could buy the factory a few times over.

Wealthy people work to earn money to pay for investments that will pay for their future. Poor people work to earn money to live everyday, thus having a survival mindset.

Wealthy people see every dollar as a seed that can produce a hundredfold. They always think, "Which share can be bought, which treasury bill?" Poor people work hard, they keep on at it forever.

Wealthy people keep on learning. Poor people think they already know.

There is a great wealth transfer. The transformation of your mind and the management of it is one of the greatest assets you can ever own because it will help you to be not a spectator but to participate in this prophetic future.

What you want to do therefore is to begin to change the way you think in order to experience the wealth transfer.

*Finally brothers whatever is true whatever is noble whatever is right whatever is pure whatever is lovely whatever is admirable-if anything is excellent or praiseworthy-think about such things.*
*Philippians 4:8*

Once your thoughts change your life will change and the finances that come into your hand will. You will see yourself as part of God's agents for creating a new world. You will not go down with every negative thing which happens, rather you will believe that God will cause unforeseen incidents, meetings and material assistance to flow in your direction.

# EIGHT CIRCLES OF WEALTH CREATION

The American Heritage Dictionary of the English language defines full circle as going back to one's starting point. One of its definitions of circle is a series or process that finishes at its starting point or continuously repeats itself as in a cycle.

The formation years of human beings are very powerful. Such periods set in stone what the life of the individual will be. It does not change unless an external message or force works so strongly upon them, thus transforming their mind from their previous conditioning; i.e. when a person gets to be born again and understands the transforming power of the Gospel of Jesus Christ.

Other than that, they go on to replicate the setting of their upbringing. And so the circle or cycle of what their parents were and possibly their grandparents and great grandparents continues with them.

A person born in the circle of poverty goes on and recreates that very experience. The nature of your family could even determine how well you master their background.

## 1. The fear based family

If you were born in a fear based family, you were not encouraged to try anything because of the fear of failure. The atmosphere in such a home makes decisions, that which you do not attempt because you do not want to make the wrong decision.

## 2. The controlling home

Those who were raised in this context were never allowed

to really fully mature in certain aspects of life. Their parents did everything for them and they go on to repeat the same thing with their children. When opportunities come their way, they shirk away from it because they were controlled all their lives.

## 3. The insecure family

The insecure family could be where children are raised in the atmosphere of separation, divorce or constant fights. In such a home, money is a problem. There is never enough of it so the children always feel financially insecure. With that kind of a mindset it becomes very difficult for them to know how to create and perpetuate wealth. Rather they create the opposite and perpetuate it.

An element of wealth creation is risk taking but once raised in a home where there is such insecurity, you are warned against taking risks.

## 4. The performance based families

In performance based families, it is more like scoring marks for every action carried out in the home. The children live to please the parent and always seek approval because they found it to be the only way they got what they needed.

They never learnt to build and not fall apart with any failure.

## 5. The abusive family

When people are raised in an abusive atmosphere - sexual, emotional or physical - they also acquire a certain addiction or taste with the experience of abuse.

Wealth creation becomes difficult because in most cases, such abuse also require an expenditure of the little funds they have.

Those who are raised in performance based homes are always seeking approval and permission before they carry out the dreams and visions they have. The nature of the financially successful is that they never wait for people's permission to go out, take risks and make it happen.

This kind of home conditions the individual and makes them feel that they deserve the poverty they have. Wealth creation becomes difficult because the mind has already been conditioned.

The belief system which works in us is always on two levels - the conscious intellectual level and the subconscious preconditioned level.

When the good news of Jesus Christ comes into you, it immediately affects your conscious, spiritual and intellectual level. However, unless there is a deliberate step to see that your mind is transformed, your subconscious preconditioned mind tends to hold sway when certain truths come in.

This is why Paul said that there has to be a renewal of the mind.

*Do not conform any longer to the pattern of this world but be transformed by the renewing of your mind. Then you will be able to test and approve what God's will is-his good pleasing and perfect will. Romans 12:2*

Take for example: as a young child, I was raised under the impression that the harder the work, the more money you make.

Later in life it made me question people who sat behind a desk and made more money than the blue collar man who spent hours and hours working in the workshops of the same company and made less than the man who came in pristine and clean clothes and sat behind the table.

The views we hold on finance, wealth creation or the realities of poverty are often shaped by our upbringing.

Having a background of poverty made me to believe the following:

**1.** That money was not common, it was always scarce

**2.** That money only comes at the end of the month

As the son of a soldier who waited until the month's end, and most of the time the money was spent in advance anyway, I grew with the belief that money was only available at the end of the month.

Our conditioned mind also made us resent those who were wealthy because we believed that all money was dirty and that you could not make a honest dollar.

My recollection of early childhood was of a home where my father always believed that one day, he would be wealthy. This is reflected in my surname which really is not the family name but my father adopted it as a positive confession that one day he would be wealthy. But he did not change the way he was conditioned by his poor father and with his capacity to increase his finance limited by both his belief system and environment he passed on the same to us.

**3.** We also believed that money could not come freely, is not easily kept and may not multiply.

We looked for quick ways to make it happen. My father spent all his 22 years in the military gambling with the hope that one day, he would make quick money.

There is a need to break free from the conditioning that has previously taken place. There is a need to get on the circles of wealth creation.

The eight circles are:

1.    Knowledge
2.    Commitment
3.    Investment
4.    Portfolio Management
5.    Wealth
6.    Reinvestment
7.    Multi-Generational Wealth
8.    Giving

We will now consider each of these circles in turn.

CIRCLE 1:

# KNOWLEDGE

E verything you know or believe about money did not come to you at birth. You were conditioned in your attitude towards finance as you grew in your family or in the environment of your upbringing.

Until the knowledge you have of finance is the appropriate one for wealth creation, every plan you have gets messed up by the disjointed opinions you hold.

Every time you want to create wealth you might find at

the back of your mind things rising against it, thus causing you to make excuses and reject what finances are coming your way.

So if you think that money is scarce, evil, bad, or dirty it will be hard for money to come to you until you get the right education. In my book, "The 10Ms of Money" I indicated the need for financial knowledge:[4]

## "Become financially literate

When I was in primary two my teacher taught us a song. The summary of it was, "Money was made to be spent." That seed sown into my heart was the only financial education I had in the whole of my school days. With such misinformation, a shaky foundation was laid for a life that was lacking in financial intelligence.

**a.** To be financially mis-educated is to make statements like "I will never be rich."

**b.** It is to be taught to write good resumés and to find a good job, not to create one.

**c.** Financial mis-education will teach you to write strong business proposals that will create jobs for others and profit for companies, and not have to create something for your future. When we were young, the few instructions we were given regarding finance were only negative warnings. We were reminded, "Money does not grow on trees." We were warned not to get into any form of indebtedness including investment.

**d.** The financially illiterate are always reacting emotionally, not working with financial intelligence. As

[4] Matthew Ashimolowo, The 10Ms of Money, England, 2003, pg.281-285

we have said in other chapters every time you allow your emotions to do your financial thinking you are likely to make mistakes.

**e.** Multiplying money requires that you be adequately informed and continue to inform yourself on how to make money and see it increase.

You must ask yourself how you will put your brain to work instead of asking how you can afford things. Educate your mind to know that being poor and being broke are not the same thing. If you are broke it is a temporary thing, but poverty is a forever problem until you break its power as we have seen under the chapter relating to mindsets. You must educate yourself to know that multiplying money is necessary because money is a form of power and once you have it you have the ability to respond.

*A feast is made for laughter and wine maketh merry: but money answereth all things. Ecclesiastes 10:19*

**f.** You must understand your need to be informed on matters of money; your need to be informed on stocks, investments, commodities and purchasing because it makes you victorious, particularly in areas where people would want you to be ignorant. Your understanding of money gives you the confidence to know that even if you are lacking in supply you would have developed the skill for making more and therefore you are not afraid. You just know the right step to take to make more.

**g.** You must inform your mind to know that it is not enough to just think positively but rather to be educated to know how to make money.

**h.** Educate your mind on how to multiply what is in your hand instead of being angry with your boss, job or spouse.

**i.** Educate your mind to go for the best to invest until you break through, to fight until you win and to give it all it takes to make a difference.

**j.** Educate your mind to use the ideas being dropped in your mind to solve problems instead of always looking to just get a job.

**k.** Educate your mind on how to put your money to work. One of the characteristics of the wealthy is that even while they are not at work their money is at work either in some company in which they have bought shares or some investment in which they have made a commitment. And believe me they watch carefully before they make such investments because only a fool and his money are soon parted.

**l.** If you have to go to financial seminars that you hear of in town, if you have to go to real estate seminars or any area of interest that increases your financial capabilities, do so. Make sure you do not stay ignorant. You can never rise beyond the level of understanding you have in any given area. You cannot walk with a light that is not available to you.

**m.** Educate your mind and allow the knowledge you gain to make you passionate, to make you desirous to win and to provoke a godly anger in you.

**n.** Educate your mind not to have to work to make money but to only work because you love to.

**o.** Educate your mind to know that part of true wealth making is to find one thing you love to do, that you are passionate about and be willing to work at that thing even if they would not pay you for it.

**p.** Educate your mind and continue the process even if it takes a lifetime to master the area of your specialty. Just stay at it; in the words of Nike "Just Do It".

**q.** Educate your mind to recognise that money is neutral; it is a tool in your hand for achieving your purpose. You must not bow at the altar of mammon but rather money must work for you.

*No man can serve two masters: for either he will hate the one and love the other; or else he will hold to the one and despise the other. Ye cannot serve God and mammon. Matthew 6:24*

**r.** You must make yourself priceless so that no one can own your soul and no employer can buy you.

**s.** Part of the process of education is to get professionals to advise you and ensure that they are worth the amount you pay them. Do not go for cheap ones but rather even if it costs a lot to hear a man speak into your life, just ensure that what is shared will make you move forward in your ability to multiply money.

There are people who are slaves to money, who obey it and do what it wants. But there are those who by reason of insight and enough educating of their minds have learnt to use money and multiply it. You must join the latter group by seeking for every insight and knowledge that makes you multiply it and not make it a master. Inform your mind; what is in your head determines what comes to your hand. So stop playing and start working. Do not live in denial. Recognise mistakes you have made and recognise what steps are to be taken to get into all that you want and all that you have to be.

Jesus told the parable of the men with talents. This story is a lesson in educating one's mind. The master of these men knew them and their ability. He knew who had the capacity to manage only one, who had the capacity to manage two and five respectively. The ones who had the ability to manage it put their money in places of upward investment and assets while the man who did not know how to manage hid it and turned such a great investment into a liability.

Certainly by the time he brought it out when the master had come, it had not retained its original value. If it were in today's world it would have actually fallen below its true value because of the rate of inflation in certain economies. We do not know but this man may have been a victim or product of today's kind of schools that are designed to produce employees, not employers - the financially illiterate, not the financially literate.

t. It is important to gain all insight on finance that will make your money multiply so that as we earlier said, you can leave something for your family.

u. Educating your mind includes learning to calculate what your money is making wherever it is and moving it if it is not multiplying. That is what makes a difference between the rich and the poor. Poor people gather around themselves what only consumes from them: cars, furniture, electronics, clothing, credit card debts and other challenges, while the truly wealthy continue to increase their earning capacity by putting much of what they have in asset building ventures."[4]

You must keep learning for the rest of your life, building your financial knowledge and expertise, acquiring the knowledge in different aspects of the financial world. In other words, learning how to read a financial statement, how to understand a prospectus or putting money to work for you.

The reason of course is that the more you know about money the better you will be able to use and control it to achieve your objectives.

The more you know about finances the more you come to that understanding that it is really a tool which can easily come into one's hand and there is no mystery to it.

[4] Matthew Ashimolowo, The 10Ms of Money, MAMM, London, 2003, pg.281-285

"Academic qualifications are important and so is financial education. They are both important and schools are forgetting one of them." - **Robert Kiyosaki**

..................................................

"Money is kind of a base subject. Like water, food, air and housing, it affects everything; yet for some reason the world of academics thinks it is a subject below their social standing." - **Robert Kiyosaki**

..................................................

"We go to school to learn to work hard for money. I write books and create products that teach people how to have money work hard for them." - **Robert Kiyosaki**

..................................................

"Your earning ability today is largely dependent upon your knowledge, skill and your ability to combine that knowledge and skill in such a way that you contribute value by which customers are going to pay." - **Brian Tracey**

..................................................

"You can't know it all, no matter how smart you are, no matter how comprehensive your education, no matter how wide ranging your experience, there is simply no way to acquire all the wisdom you need to make your business thrive." - **Donald Trump**

..................................................

"Financial education needs to become a part of our national curriculum and scoring systems so that it is not just the rich kids that learn about money, it is all of us." - **David Bach**

**CIRCLE 2:**

# COMMITMENT

The human mind is very interesting. Once it has been elasticated it never goes back to its original condition. With financial knowledge acquired, the next step is a commitment.

There is always a way out for the person who is committed to the cause he pursues.

Commitment must be accentuated, not by speeches but by:

## a. A game plan

Wealthy people would not have become who they are by chance, but by taking tangible actions.

In other words there is a precise and methodological approach. Do not forget that as a believer you have the advantage of the prophecy having gone forth but how beautiful it is. Prophecies find fulfilment when the individuals are themselves prepared. In my book, 101 Great Laws of Success, the Law of Preparation says,

"Preparation enhances performance, increases confidence. It creates the atmosphere for the seed of faith to germinate."[5]

*But sanctify the Lord God in your hearts: and be ready always to give an answer to every man that asketh you a reason of the hope that is in you with meekness and fear.  1 Peter 3: 15*

If you must leave where you are to go to where you ought, there has to be a clear map. The beauty of driving with a modern car today is that when you set the GSPS (Global Satellite Positioning System), fully indicating where you are going, the map and the voice take you where you are going no matter how far and how complicated the journey is.

In the same vein, there can be a clear map of where you want to go in your financial life. Your plan must first of all audit where you are now - if you are at a loss, having assets or liabilities. It should then be followed with a plan indicating a start point and an end date.

Maybe you want to set a goal, that at the end of 12 cal-

[5] Matthew Ashimolowo, 101 Great Laws of Success, MAMM, London, 1999

endar months you will have come out of poverty and built enough baseline for wealth creation. If you have debts, part of your plan should be how to erase your debt. We will talk more of debt when we come to the third circle of wealth creation.

You need to ask yourself frank questions:

1.  What do you want in your financial life?

2.  What gift and/ or ability do you have that can produce this wealth?

3.  What are the current liabilities you have?

4.  What are the other money consuming ventures, activities or situations you have on your hand?

5.  What is your monthly income?

6.  What is your expenditure?

7.  Do you have any assets? - An asset is that which retains value.

8.  Are you desperate enough to come out of poverty? Are you desperate enough to be used of God as a millionaire for advancing His Kingdom?

The eight questions raised must not be read and passed over. You need to stop and do due diligence on the state of your financial affairs. Unless this is properly done, every other exercise will be futile.

## b. Commitment is leadership

You may want to use other people in the process of the creation of wealth. You may trust in your banker to explain the best savings and investments plans to you or your broker to show you which companies you should buy shares in. However, if you really must get into the kind of wealth we are talking about here, you would have to take the lead yourself. You would have to follow the process and be passionate about your dream. No one feels your situation like you do.

# INVESTMENT

**O**nce your commitment towards creation is established the next thing is to start the journey in investment.

This must always be done by working with your strength. Your strength is meant to give birth to what will be your core product. One of the reasons why you must work in your strength is because satan always tries to delude your life with options.

Options sometimes break people's focus and make them lose their primary calling. Your core product is what will end up as that by which you shall be remembered.

When investing in your strength, it can either be with what you already know or in an area where you require new skills. If I am a computer software programmer and now want to create wealth through farming, it is possible; however it means that I am depending on newly acquired skills. This may mean taking a little longer than I may have set out in my time plan.

The key for creating wealth is to first start with the abilities which you can turn on and begin to create wealth within a few weeks.

## DEBT MANAGEMENT

Of all the money mistakes, the most major for the modern man is going into debt. There are people who spend 20 per cent of their income servicing the debt they have. They cannot afford to be without a job or a business. In the words of the poor: "I owe, I owe and so to work I go."

We will cover indebtedness more closely. However, once you launch yourself on an ocean of red ink, buying things you cannot pay for and having lines of credit for everything, it means you are living beyond your means and are spending the money you have not earned.

Indebtedness is often rooted in a person's sense of compulsion to buy, and with today's easy availability of credit facilities people see what they like, and because the price seems right they bring out their credit cards and buy, unknown to them that they may be clearing the path to poverty. Going into debt is an indirect training for your children to follow the same.

*The rich ruleth over the poor, and the borrower is servant to the lender. Proverbs 22:7*

In the previous verse the Bible says, "train up a child in the way he should go."

*Train up a child in the way he should go: and when he is old he will not depart from it. Proverbs 22:6*

So your child observes you and sees your actions. Borrowing is the father of bankruptcy. Once it is not controlled, bankruptcy will look you in the face. Indebtedness is an evil spirit that has your destruction as its ultimate goal. Those who provide credit facilities prefer you to borrow because it helps the economy and helps their own income. So that the car you were supposed to buy for £15,000, you might end up paying £21,000 at the end of four or five years.

Debtors are presumptuous that they will have a job tomorrow.

In today's volatile world that is a tall order. Debt makes Christians forget that they are promise keepers and so when they are unable to fulfil their promise, excuses are given and sometimes lies are told to cover their tracks.

A greater percentage of those that draw the equity on their house often use it to pay off debts they owe; whereas those who create wealth will take the equity to start a new business or buy more real estate.

You cannot really overcome indebtedness unless you are realistic about your income and how much of it is available to you. Imagine a man who earns £12,000 and pays 25 per cent in tax, 7 per cent in national insurance, 17.5 per cent value added tax on all purchases except for the children's clothing and a few of the necessities we buy. In a nutshell, out of 12 months income only eight months income really stays with you. So if you earn £12,000, what is really available to you is £8,000.

Remember also that out of the £8,000, £1,200 belongs to the Lord in the tithe. This leaves the believer with £6,800. Ignorance of these facts will make indebtedness spread faster than any disease, it will make such a person groan every time they want to give to God because they calculate what 10 per cent (the tithe) now means to them forgetting that the Government did not ask permission before it withdrew its own 32 per cent in income tax and national insurance contributions.

Indebtedness makes some well-meaning couples struggle in spite of the level of wages they earn.

Having bought most of the things in their house on credit, unpaid bills now stay on their mind like a bad dream. They walk on carpets that are 'buy now pay later', they drive a car that is on a similar arrangement, their home is mortgaged, the television they watch is bought on credit, they patronise catalogues and brochures of shopping companies that allow you to buy and spread the payment over years. The result is family tension and constant arguments.

Indebtedness also drains the joy out of payday.

It has meant that some people have eaten the tithe and money that belongs to God. Lies and deception are easier for debtors than those who are debt free. Confidence is eroded when you are a debtor, particularly when you see the people you owe. Indebtedness makes you enslaved to the system of the world.

The Word says, "borrowers are servants of lenders." The major reason for work then becomes paying all your lenders, ensuring that you keep them happy so they do not come and use the long arm of the law to take everything you have. Most western nations have so empowered lenders to recover their money by using the long arm of the law, even if it means throwing you out of your accommodation and repossessing everything you have worked for to pay off the money you owe.

Indebtedness may cause the courts to determine what you spend your money on, in other words a counsellor may have to be hired to budget your own income for you, and such a counsellor may decide that you have no right to bring the tithe. The 'buy now pay later' marketing strategy of this world enslaves you and your children.

Of course there is the time to use debt but only as leverage for a business so that you are using other people's money to perpetuate and produce more money. As a result, your children are being raised in the atmosphere of debt and when you bring up your children as debtors, you have disobeyed the Lord.

*Train up a child in the way he should go: and when he is old he will not depart from it. Proverbs 22:6*

Children catch behaviours and children also go forth and perpetuate what they have seen you do. Borrowing is the guaranteed passport to financial slavery. The rich rule over the poor and the borrower is servant to the lender.

*The rich ruleth over the poor, and the borrower is servant to the lender. Proverbs 22:7*

Unless there is a change, generation upon generation will be held in financial bondage. So while the righteous man leaves an inheritance for his grandchildren, the debtor leaves challenges, battles and heartache for their spouse and relations.

*A good man leaveth an inheritance to his children's children; and the wealth of the sinner is laid up for the just. Proverbs 13:22*

*Now there cried a certain woman of the wives of the sons of the prophets unto Elisha, saying, Thy servant my husband is dead; and thou knowest that thy servant did fear the Lord; and the creditor is come to take unto him my two sons to be bondmen.*
*2 Kings 4:1*

The indebtedness of the prophet, which he left for his wife and sons, added burdens, multiplied their worries, subtracted their peace and divided their minds.

He now left his wife worried because the only thing he left in the world for her, her sons, were about to be taken by the people who provided the credit facilities.

Indebtedness produces sleepless nights and makes people question your integrity.

It makes you feel the grind of borrowing on the inside.

Indebtedness embarrasses you particularly when you are behind in your payments. It can lead to family acrimony. Indebtedness makes you not look forward to the postman bringing your letters because another reminder might be on the way.

Indebtedness invites the spirit of fear into your home so that you are no longer at peace but perpetually afraid of what might happen to you and your family.

Indebtedness takes away confidence and makes the man feel inadequate as a provider for his family. Indebtedness leaves your family stressed because any little wastage by your children makes you over-react over 'spilled milk.'

Debt between friends is another great challenge that causes the separation of friends. Imagine borrowing your friend's car and just as you were coming back from your trip, someone who was driving dented a part of it. Having no money to repair it, you had to take it and explain. The reaction of the friend immediately changes because what is important to them has been tampered with. The spirit of debt is a bad master; it rules and it ruins.

Indebtedness can frustrate the vision of a church.

People have been tempted to steal, therefore losing their job or even facing the possibility of a jail sentence because of indebtedness. Technically, the lender determines the movement of a borrower. They determine where you may go, what you may do and how you may spend. So when a debtor is led by the Holy Spirit to give a certain amount, the first thing he remembers is his line of credit which must not be jeopardised and so he faces the temptation of disobeying the Holy Spirit thus being rendered useless in the promotion of the Kingdom of God with his income.

Indebtedness really does frustrate one's destiny because the calling on the believer is to go out and make money in order to use it to promote the Kingdom of God. However, the rich who rule over the poor are now taking it.

People who get into indebtedness presume or forecast the future.

They presume that the current value of their house is a certain amount and is likely to increase.

They fail to realise that things could happen and there could be calamities or disasters in the area where they live.

In summary debt is a thief that robs one of his time and life. It is like being enslaved again to serve people you owe. It is the transfer of the wealth of the poor to the wealthy. Somebody somewhere is spending your money because you have chosen to walk in indebtedness. So if you cannot imagine Jesus in debt, then it is not the lifestyle you should follow.

You must create a method for eliminating all your debts. This starts with a listing of all those who are your creditors, the amount you owe them, how much you are willing to put aside regularly to pay them off. Where it is a commercial debt which has interest on it, paying off the principal and the interest is vital.

There are people who sometimes would have money in

savings or investments accounts while they carry debts that also have interest accruing on them. You must realise that the interest on your deposit or investment account cannot be anywhere comparable to the one on the money you borrow.

Liquidating your investment or savings account to pay off debt is a form of investment in the sense that you reduce the amount of money you owe and the length of time it takes to pay it off.

## ENTER THE PLAYING FIELD

As you enter the playing field of the investment world you come in on one of four levels - employee, self-employed, businessman or investor.

Each of these predetermines the amount of wealth you can create or manage. It is almost impossible to meet employees who are millionaires except for CEOs of multinational companies whose total package makes them millionaires.

The self-employed is a small scale player in the world of business. He determines how much business he does; however, most times he is unable to create volume even though his condition is better than that of an employee.

The businessman is one who runs businesses for profit. Such a person has a capacity to create volume, or large space and therefore create great turnovers and produce wealth.

The investor - In today's world there are men and woman who have made enough wealth to the point that all they do is invest it in other people's dreams and visions. They are able to compound the interest on their wealth as they set themselves up.

The second wealthiest man on earth, Warren Buffett, made most of his money from investment in stocks and shares.

## WAYS TO INVEST

### 1. Leveraging

This is the asset you borrow to increase your operational base. We talked earlier about indebtedness and that you must ensure that this is paid off. However, in the early days, as you begin the journey of investment you will need to create leverage for yourself, increasing your financial power or advantage through the temporary usage of other assets which you either borrowed or loaned in order to increase your effectiveness.

*Elisha said "Go around and ask all your neighbors for empty jars. Don't ask for just a few. 2 Kings 4:3*

### 2. Precious metals

These are bought and sold on the commodities markets as well as bullion markets around the world. Precious metals could be iron, aluminium, copper or tin. Precious gems, the investment in rare, delicate and precious stones, e.g. diamonds.

The sale of these gems is always controlled in order to keep their price high and increase the value for those who have invested in it.

### 3. Collectors items

These are stamps, paintings and antiques. The collection of rare items and subsequent sale when it appreciates is what we mean here. It is a potential source of capital gain and it protects your money against inflation.

### 4. Treasury bills

A treasury bill is a short term investment paid upon maturation of the bill. It is a gilt-edge security issued by governments. This form of investment is among the safest as the government is unlikely to default on interest or on principal repayment.

Treasury bills come as short term, medium and long term.

### 5. Money market funds

This is the market for short-term loans in which money brokers arrange for loans between the banks, the governments, discount houses and the accepting houses.

The main items of exchange in this transaction are bills of exchange, treasury bills and trade bills. Through a person's individual bank or investment houses they can place deposits in the money market at a higher rate of interest than they could have received in the common deposit account.

### 6. Stocks and shares

These are one of the most popular in certain economies. They give you the opportunity to buy into companies that are publicly quoted. It is the ownership of shares or stocks in a company. The dividend received or loss experienced will be determined by the performance of the shares in the stock market.

The prices change constantly; in fact, sometimes daily. If the company does well then its shares are likely to rise and these can fall as well, so there is a risk involved.

## 7. Bonds

It is an interest bearing debt certificate issued either by a financial institutions, a government or company. It is loaning money to an entity for a defined period at a specified interest rate.

In exchange for your money, such entity issues a certificate or bond which states the interest rate, commitment and the time of payment.

## 8. Premium bonds

This is a bond that is valued at more than its face value. A discount bond is one sold below its face value. Bonds are usually sold against loans, mortgages, credit card income etc. as marketable securities and commodities.

## 9. Commodities

These are elements of economic wealth which can be bought or sold. Raw materials can be traded on the commodity market - grain, coffee, cocoa, wool, cotton, rubber, potbellies or oranges - and they are sometimes known as soft commodities.

Sometimes metals and solid raw materials known as hard

commodities can be traded on the commodities market. This was the method by which Joseph, in the Bible became a millionaire. He traded in commodities.

## 10. Mutual trust funds

A mutual fund is money committed to a portfolio manager who buys and sells stocks to make profit for you. It is sometimes also called unit trust. It is a special method that enables the investors to pool their resources together, several people putting their money in one pot through a broker. It helps to spread the risk and to use professional advice and management.

## 11. General business

This is the act of buying and selling or carrying out a particular service for financial returns.

*Do you see a man skilled in his work? He will serve before kings; he will not serve before obscure men. Proverbs 22:29*

## 12. Retirement funds also known as pension funds

By contributing to a pension scheme in a lot of economies you attract a tax relief at the maximum interest rate available.

## 13. The creation of a cash cow

The creation of a cash cow is very central to wealth creation. This is what will continue to supply life to the wealth circle. It comes from your capacity to continue to create more revenue from one of the investment methods or businesses you venture into.

The business venture you engage in combined with the skills you have. It is what makes your cash cow. Such business has to be real, not a dream, so that you can establish your working cash cow.

As you are gaining more experience in the process of wealth creation, what we are saying in effect is - imagine a mathematics teacher who wants to create wealth. He would have to maybe establish a company by which he runs coaching classes and therefore charges outside of the school where he earns his salary. He has immediately created a cash cow. If he coaches 100 children at a rate of £10 per hour, that is £1,000. Imagine if he runs maybe ten of these in a month. The total would be £10.000. That cash cow is already yielding its milk.

The teacher will need to sit down and write a vision for his coaching classes, his strategy and tactics for running it as a business showing a revenue model which will be his target. He will have a marketing plan for selling the coaching class to parents and his students, and therefore take the lead.

My favourite cash cow is real estate and in order for you to grasp what I am trying to say, I will give you reasons why I believe in real estate.

## 14. Real estate investment

This is one of the areas where initial investment is not excessively large yet with time, it brings a large yield. It is the buying and selling of land and houses. People will always need somewhere to live. The majority of new families will start with rented places.

The property market itself is susceptible to changes like others but the formula for making it happen is the same - passive inflow of income. Once one of these methods of income is adopted, with time it creates a passive inflow of income. That is, the interest or profit which comes from engaging in any form of investment.

Wisdom therefore will be to reinvest such funds. We shall look at this in more details.

**Why real estate?**[6]

**1.** You can recover from mistakes.

**2.** You can work with other people's money.

**3.** It is easier to multiply your investment.

**4.** Value can increase with minimal investment.

**5.** Benefits can be drawn through a re-mortgage without selling.

**6.** Unlike the stock exchange you do not need to monitor how a property is doing on a minute by minute basis.

**7.** It is not easily dated. Most investments are dated.

**8.** Real estate has every sign of perpetuating.

**9.** While shares may be passed down, in one slump of the market it could be wiped out.

**10.** There are times when there is a slump in real estate, but even at such times it is still relatively better than the other investments at maintaining income.

[6] 101 Insights on Real Estate, Coming Publication of MAMM

**11.** It requires probably less intellectual input compared to the other forms of investment but more leg work.

**12.** Most wealthy people keep their wealth in real estate.

**13.** Your own money in real estate investment may be a fraction of the total worth.

**14.** Financial institutions are ready to make lines of credit available for real estate, not for the purchase of diamonds, antiques, mutual funds or bond certificates.

**15.** It is considered one of the most secure investments you could ever make.

**16.** Banks hardly give you a loan to invest in shares but cannot wait to give you money if you come to them with a good plan for purchasing real estate.

**17.** The interest rates on mortgages are generally lower than business loans.

**18.** Real estate is attractive to banks because lending can be tied to the property you are getting a mortgage on.

**19.** Real estate value does not plummet to the level which shares fall.

**20.** House prices rise along with their peers.

**21.** Most investments require a lot of information, education and acquisition of skill in that chosen field.

**22.** Dealing in real estate requires a handful of insight on where to buy, what to buy, when to buy and how to wait for the right deal.

**23.** Most disasters do not totally wipe away property values and moreover you can insure against such disasters.

**24.** By the end of the eighth year of setting up companies 80 per cent of such companies fail or fold up. If the same kind of money used in the set up of the company is invested in real estate the property would still be there.

**25.** There is hardly any nation, continent or city where real estate does not do relatively well.

**Taking smart actions on real estate**

**26.** Do not pay the standard variable rate for a mortgage - negotiate.

**27.** Do not change mortgage lenders if you can save thousands when buying a latter property from the one on which you had a previous mortgage.

**28.** Find out if by switching to another lender before your fixed term is over you will still pay less monthly payments despite the penalties.

**29.** It is no crime to ring your lenders and ask if there is a deal that will save you money.

**30.** Go for capped rates without redemption penalties.

**31.** It is better to go for products without redemption penalties.

**32.** Search for lenders who may want to cover valuation and legal fees, or alternatively who may give a large discount.

**33.** Every £100 paid in excess on a fixed monthly payment mortgage equals to £313 or minus two weeks off the total you are supposed to pay.

## How to manage real estate

**34.** Do not insist on investing on properties in your locality out of sentiment. If it becomes necessary to move into another area, go ahead and do it.

**35.** Consider letting out the old house or apartment as you move to the new.

**36.** Never keep a building empty. Let your money keep working for you while you go to bed.

**37.** Do not let out your property without informing your mortgagors.

**38.** Beware of letting agents if you can.

**39.** Your insurers will need to know that you are letting out.

**40.** House prices can fall. Stop borrowing all the time on the equity of your house unless it is to create leverage for other investments.

**41.** Make sure there is a good demand before you get involved in a 'buy-to-let' deal.

**42.** Make higher repayments when you borrow against your home.

**43.** Always compare mortgage rates offered by different institutions.

**44.** Do not be carried away by interior décor when buying properties. Check for signs of ageing and of building problems.

**45.** Aim to pay earlier than the number of years on the mortgage.

**46.** Except for the situation where you keep using other people's money to create leverage to create more money, it is wiser to see that the mortgage on the immediate house in which you live is cleared.

**47.** Make efforts to pay before the monthly due date on the mortgage.

**48.** When looking for properties consider the location. It is very important to recognise that the property does not always stand alone.

**49.** Endeavour to cut down your monthly outlay of payments by having more than the 5 per cent deposit required.

**50.** Do not go for a leasehold. Only do it if it is an investment property.

**51.** Check the terms of the contract if it is leasehold so that there are no caveats and conditions that make it onerous and impossible to do anything with the property.

**52.** Check for infestation of ants, rodents and cockroaches. This makes the property hard to sell.

**53.** Ensure that there are no covenants or charges on the land.

**54.** Do not set out to build overseas unless you can supervise the work.

**55.** Do not invest in real estate overseas unless you are going to use it and it should be where properties appreciate.

**56.** Look for properties that require little work, renovate and sell.

**57.** If you live overseas be wise with your method of sending money for property purchase.

**58.** Always view real estate as an upward investment.

**59.** Real estate could be a means of generating income without much effort.

**60.** Avoid enticing mortgage schemes that have long-term drawbacks.

**61.** Do not succumb to estate agents languages of pressure.

**62.** Know other extra costs in the area - property tax, association tax as it is called in America, insurance, land costs and land tax.

**63.** View your intended property during the daytime so that all is revealed and nothing takes you by surprise after the purchase.

**64.** The crime rate in an area can affect your home and content insurance. It is important to do a demographic survey of the area where you are investing.

**65.** Ask for a mortgage with daily interest rate calculation.

**66.** If in doubt about the quality of a building, pay for a full structural survey.

**67.** Survey the building for subsidence or flooding if necessary.

**68.** Avoid co-ownership and housing trusts of associations if you can. It limits your own equity although it gives you an opportunity to start up.

**69.** The range of local authority services available to you must be checked and verified.

**70.** Avoid listed buildings unless you are ready for the restrictions.

**71.** If you are selling remember that every little work carried out will enhance the quality of your property.

**72.** When buying investment properties try for a low deposit mortgage.

**73.** First time buyers should find a mortgage before finding a property.

**74.** Sign on with agents who have the kind of property you want.

**75.** Do not wait for agents to send you details, pursue them.

**76.** If you are buying a house or property at the auctions, your limitations are many.

**77.** Therefore the counsel would be to inspect the property before the auction day where possible to ensure that as much as possible you do not inherit tenants who could cause all kinds of problems (encumbrance etc.)

**78.** Buy homes at the bottom end of the market; most of them just need a simple face-lift.

**79.** A one bedroom flat is ideal to quickly rent out. One or two bedroom apartments are always a winner. There is always someone somewhere looking for such apartments.

**80.** When buying from auctions, make an offer before it is published.

**81.** The rent and the mortgage of small apartments are usually in line with each other.

**82.** Look at the house from the point of view of the tenants - the house you are buying on auction for rent.

**83.** Real estate does not lose its value as soon as you get home.

**84.** Real estate increases your asset base.

**85.** Real estate may be slow but continues to keep your money working for you.

**86.** Real estate makes money your employee that goes to work while you are asleep.

**87.** Get your finances in order:

The way your money is being spent is an indication of your ability to manage the funding of a property. It is no use taking a mortgage if you have not been able to discipline yourself with your income and expenditure.

The word 'mortgage' itself comes from two Latin words - mort which stands for death and gage which stands for level. So a mortgage is more or less the level of your death.

If you can't manage finances very well, your debt level remains for long.

**88.** Start searching early for the house:

Do not wait until the last minute before you start searching for the property you need. Therefore you should use every avenue. Surf the net, check with realtors and let friends know you are looking. Use all methods you can to search.

**89.** Only use the services of a good real estate agent:

Every good business enterprise has its *mickey mouse and sharks*. It is very important for you to use the services of the ones who know their onions, who will give you the best service for your money.

**90.** Keep abreast of the financial industry:

If you are going to take a loan, a mortgage to buy a property you need to be aware of the various fundings available, the benefits that are going to be passed on to you, which lender will serve your need.

There are times when in certain societies specialised lenders work with people. There are lenders who cater specifically for students, single parents, older people etc.

**91.** Get a mortgage offer:

Get a mortgage offer before you go too far in settling for a property. Do not search and agree before you look for a lender. You do not want to get stuck or find that the property which you found passed on to someone else because you could not come up with finances.

**92.** Before you say, "I do":

Before you take on the property, ensure that you have looked at it, particularly areas that are likely to bring down the value of the property. This may require the use of an expert surveyor who knows what to look for, search for cracks, dents, the growth of fungi at the base of the building and paintings that attempt to possibly hide the weakness of the property.

Ask for certificates that cover things like the dampness and woodwork.

**93.** Make the offer

Once you are satisfied with the quality of the building, taking into account the location, beauty, aesthetics, the surrounding neighbours, the quality of the building, you can then make your offer.

Always make an offer that leaves potential equity in the building you buy so if the building were say, $100,000, make all efforts to get it at $90,000 or $95,000. It is unwise and bad business to start in a zero equity atmosphere. It will mean that the first few payments you are making are made into a zero investment situation.

**94.** Watch out for last minute problems:

Even great experts on real estate do make mistakes at the last minute. However, as you keep learning, you keep correcting. One of the mistakes is to start the process of purchasing without covering yourself with insurance.

If you buy property in the United Kingdom there is what is called 'exchange of contract' and then the 'completion'. When contracts are exchanged you have made a commitment to buy, awaiting the final transfer of money from you to the vendor. Were there to be fire in the building after contracts have been exchanged, you are committed to buy. That is why it is wiser to protect the building with insurance for a couple of hundreds of dollars or pounds.

I know one or two cases where people have bought buildings and the contracts had not been completed when vandals set fire to the building. Of course the vendors insisted that the vendor must complete it because they committed to purchasing.

Another benefit of the insurance is that, were you to change your mind at the very last minute or unable to go on with the completion, the insurance may protect you until you dispose of the building if you were no longer using it.

**95.** Do not buy a building without inspecting:

One of the men who gave Jesus an excuse for not coming to the banquet, said that he was going to inspect a land he was buying. That was foolishness because to inspect a piece of land at night was to expose yourself to the chance of buying land that is unusable.

In England for example there is land we call 'brownfield.' This is land where certain chemicals have been used in processing and production and therefore would require hundreds of thousands of pounds to clean such chemicals from the land.

It may also be eco-sensitive land that is not allowed for building. More so if it is a building, there may be other issues which cannot be seen during the night or that are not obvious, to even the most prying eyes.

You will therefore require, along with a surveyor, a proper inspection of such building.

**96.** Plan your payment:

The mistake is to make inadequate plans for the monthly payment of the money you have borrowed. It is not too long before the euphoria of purchasing a house is over. If you have done a good job of planning how to pay, it will become obvious when the mortgagers come calling.

**97.** Ensure that all agreements are in writing:

Make sure all aspects of the contract are in black and white. The buying of a building is not what you do by a viva voce (verbal yes). What you are willing to do or not do must be clear in writing so that you are not buying based on good intentions.

**98.** Do not miss the *small print:*

I know it is not popular for many who are in a hurry to read small print which lawyers write. However, with real estate, because it will be with you for years and it is also a major financial commitment, it is very wise to read the smallest of print because it can be inserted in your nice documents statements that restrict movement, light, air, views, rent etc.

There are properties that already have restrictive covenants as to who you can sell unto when you are ready to dispose. I recall many years ago when our church wanted to buy a small football field for our future church building. Only to find in the covenant that restricts the sale of the land only to those who will use it as a small midtown farm. You may need the services of your lawyers to make sense of the *small print.*

**99.** Do not carry too much debt:

Mortgages are often based on a person's salary; however, with today's cut throat, competitive market mortgagers are also willing and ready to look the other way once they find people who want to borrow.

Sometimes people have managed to find 20 to 30 per cent of the value of the mortgage or the property. Once you are able to put 30 per cent down, most mortgagers in Europe and America will not ask further questions.

However, as the one who will have to face the debt remember the mortgage is the level of your death. Carrying a heavy mortgage is predicting your own demise.

**100.** Do the final checks:

When people have experienced the debilitating disease of cancer and go through a period of healing and chemotherapy, they still keep going for the final check to be sure that there is no more trace.

When buying a building, there is need for that final check, going through with a fine-tooth comb to ensure nothing is missing because the purchase of a building is more complex than the legality of a marriage. In marriage there are now people taking on a divorce certificate. However, once a building is bought and the contract is completed, there is nowhere else to turn so it is important to do it right from the beginning.[6]

---

[6] 101 Insights on Real Estate, Coming Publication of MAMM

# CIRCLE 4:
# PORTFOLIO MANAGEMENT

The fourth step in the circle of wealth creation is the management of the portfolio you have now created by the investments you are involved in. It is this act of management that will determine how your wealth increases.

Managing wealth could be through the engagement of the services of specialists as in a stock broker, bank manager or financial services adviser that are champions. We earlier referred to advisers who would help in the management of wealth. It is impossible to do without a team around you if you would break from the levels of mere earning to the realm of wealth creation.

You need to assemble a team who would help you on your way to succeeding. There is no doubt the Holy Spirit will lead you and guide you. However, the Bible says, "In the multitude of counsellors there is safety."

*For lack of guidance a nation falls, but many advisers make victory sure. Proverbs 11:14*

*For waging war you need guidance, and for victory many advisers. Proverbs 24:6*

You are not good at everything. We all have tunnel vision in several areas. As a matter of fact your gift tends to make you narrow your view only to the area of your strength; therefore you need to add to your team people who are good with marketing, publicity, financing, operations, distribution etc.

If like me you have real estate as your cash cow you will then need to have as advisers people who know the difference between commercial and residential properties, surveyors, architects, town planners and developers. The broader the spectrum of your investment, the more you will need to increase your mentors.

If in the process you make the mistake of choosing the wrong person, that should not discourage you. You need to look for a way out of any predicament you find yourself in and move on with your dream.

Some of these people will come through networking and the contacts you will make.

# NETWORKING

Networking is an interconnected system of things or people. It is an extended group of people with similar interests or concerns who interact and remain in informal contact or mutual assistance or support.[7]

Every favour in scripture released into individual lives came by reason of their network. Joseph did not fulfil his calling until he was in the right place.

## CREATE A COMPANY (THIRTY REASONS)

If you want to create wealth and truly become a millionaire for God you will need to begin to think and act like one. Most wealthy people, even in the secular world know that there is a need for them to create a company or companies in order to be able to effectively manage what comes into their hand.

Most wealthy people you know of and read about have multiple corporations and trusts as well as charitable organisations with which they are able to achieve more with the monies which they have generated.

There are several reasons why you should create a company, among which are the following:

### 1. Tax efficiency.

Several expenses you would have had to handle with your personal salary if you were in a job, can legally be dealt with as company expenses and this includes utilities, computer equipment, rent for office or home office deduction, phone, office supplies, employees, salaries and

[7] The American Heritage Dictionary of the English Language, 4th Edition, 2000, Houghton Mifflin Company

bonus, fees for legal accounting, bookkeeping, quoting, mentoring and contractors, gifts, corporate housing, marketing, entertainment, meals, travel, car, petrol, insurance, websites, internet education etc.

**2.** The creation of your own company provides protection against liabilities. We will have more details on this later.

**3.** Reduction of personal liabilities when you form a limited liability company (LLC).

**4.** You are able to create greater space and volume when you run a business that is through a company.

**5.** The possibility of global impact.

**6.** A company helps to concentrate your efforts through a legal entity.

**7.** This is one place where you cannot be sacked and you have permanent job security as long as the company is viable.

**8.** Anonymity.

You can buy properties and cars in the name of the company, and that way, keep your anonymity. If people want to research on you, investment properties and cars are easy ways to perform an asset search on you. When people want to initiate a lawsuit against you, it is common for them to hire a lawyer who will first perform an asset search. Once all properties and equities are owned in the name of a company you can maintain your anonymity.

**9.** Raising capital.

If you register a partnership or proprietorship, if you try to approach the bank on your individual right, there is a certain degree of capital you might be able to raise but there is a greater source of capital available to limited liability companies that are performing very well.

**10.** Separate legal entity.

You and your small business corporation, charitable organisation or trust which you form are separate legal entities. If anyone were to decide to bring lawsuits, they can bring it against your company but not you and if it was brought against you, they cannot use it in most cases to try to take over your company.

**11.** The ownership of a company means you can determine your own day off, not having to apply to anyone for it.

**12.** You are your own boss, controlling your destiny and how you run your life.

**13.** A personal company means a better life, car and vacation because the company pays for it.

**14.** A company gives you a sense of ownership, destiny and the things which you use the company to buy.

**15.** You are able to build equity into your future through a company.

Many people find that at retirement they have to now cut down and live on less.

**16.** The formation of a company means that you have the chance to build something of great value which bears your signature or name.

**17.** You can pass a company on to your children. You cannot pass your employment on to them.

**18.** A business will keep producing even in your golden years.

With jobs, when the company feels that you are no longer contributing you are likely to be retrenched, paid off or retired.

**19.** A job pays you monthly but the ownership of a company means you are paid for years of your life.

**20.** A job gives you a pay cheque, a business gives you residual income, beyond your director's salary.

**21.** Your company can exist continuously even after your death.

**22.** Through your company you have the power to enter contracts.

**23.** Your company has the power to hold, purchase and convey real estate and personal property and to mortgage and lease any such real estate to anyone you authorise.

**24.** Your company has the power to borrow money when necessary for the transactions of its business or for the exercise of its corporate rights, privileges or franchises.

**25.** Your company can reach the point where you also begin to issue bonds, promissory notes or even bills of exchanges, debentures and other obligations and evidences by which you can borrow money payable at a specific time or times.

**26.** Your company has the power to make donations to public welfare or for charitable, scientific or educational purposes.

This means in effect that once you create the wealth you can decide in your board meeting that the tithe of this company you have created and some of its profits be used for the furtherance of the Gospel and the work of ministry.

**27.** A company gives you the power to conduct business, have offices, hold purchase mortgage and convey real and personal property in other nations depending on the law of the land in which you are.

**28.** A company gives you the power to purchase, wholesale and transfer shares of its own capital stock.

**29.** When you set up a company the advantage also is that you have the power to decide when to wind up, or dissolve such a company without being wound up if you are within the law.

**30.** The ownership of a company gives you the opportunity to be able to provide employment for the unemployed, thus solving problems for others.

At the end of the nineteenth century, Henry Ford floated a company which manufactured the Ford car. As we write, over a 100 years later, there is still a Ford sitting at the helm of affairs in the company. He could have taken on a job and been forgotten but by this act he created a future and left an inheritance for his children's children.

One of the greatest companies in the United States of America, General Electric, was founded by the legendary Thomas Edison in 1882. It now stands as one of the world's largest corporations.

A group of people started a company called the Hudson Bay Company in 1670. It is still running long after they have gone. And with the availability of the internet today, you have an almost unlimited customer base, unlimited advertisement, the ability to showcase your work without being confined to the 'nine to five' mentality.

If you must be a millionaire, there is the need to own your own company.

CIRCLE 5:

# WEALTH

We come to the fifth in our circles of wealth creation.

**1.** The first argument here is that once you begin to pursue financial literacy, you are arming yourself with not just adequate information but enough knowledge to rewrite the negatives that could have been written into your mind concerning money.

**2.** The next step is commitment. No one could be as

committed as you are to your financial well-being.

**3.** Investment - whether in large or small quantity. It is your investment that begins to provide the grounds for increase and the pathway to wealth.

**4.** Portfolio management is firstly an understanding that the various platforms for investing as created by you, now need to be managed, serviced and watched over for maximisation. Once this is done it will result in wealth

The word 'wealth' has become more of anathema to some people to the extent that there is such reaction once it comes up. However, the average human being, including those who resist the word, wake up every day trying to better their own financial well-being.

## WHAT IS WEALTH?

The American Heritage Dictionary of the English language defines wealth as, "An abundance of valuable materials or resources: riches. The state of being rich: affluent, in great amounts."

The WordNet of Princeton University defines it as, "The state of being rich and affluent. Having a plentiful supply of material goods and money, an abundance of material possessions and resources."

This same dictionary goes further by defining wealth to be property that has economic utility, a monetary value or an exchange value.

Wealth in a sense is different from being rich. Riches require that you just have enough money. Once you have a million US dollars or British pounds, you are a million-aire - therefore you are rich.

But wealth goes further. It is having enough of all the essentials of life i.e. love, good health, friends and family, spirituality and of course, enough money.

There are 'Scrooges' out there who have the money but no one to share it with. There are 'Shylocks' who have made enough money but have angered enough people and now demand 'a pound of flesh without blood'.

What we are saying therefore is that being wealthy is a total package - laughter, love, living, good health, peace, money and relationships.

In a book like this, this is not a sudden downgrading of money. When people have tried to do that they have come to discover that with no money you cause yourself a lot of stress, sleepless nights, sickness, disease and really, the quality of health service you get is determined by the money you have in your purse in any economy.

> "Being rich is having money. Being wealthy is having time." - **Margaret Bonnano**
> ........................................
> "The real measure of your wealth is how much you would be worth if you lost all your money." - **Unknown**
> ........................................
> "Ordinary riches can be stolen. Real riches cannot. In your soul are infinitely precious things that cannot be taken from you." - **Oscar Wilde**

> "Prosperity is a way of living and thinking; and not just money and things. Poverty is a way of living and thinking; and not just a lack of money or things." -
> **Eric Butterworth**

Ignoring money is foolishness. You must learn to open your brains to creative solutions. Wealth as a target in itself is deceptive. You should rather pursue it in order to have enough to serve God, touch mankind, bless your community, and enjoy the life God has given you but in the end become a conduit through which God's great wealth can reach the world.

> "Wealth is not his that has it but his that enjoys it." -
> **Benjamin Franklyn**
> ....................................
> "Money is the sign of liberty. To curse money is to curse liberty--to curse life, which is nothing, if it be not free." - **de Gourmont**

What is wealth? Wealth is really all that you own after all your liabilities have been deducted. It is all the valuables you own. Again the dictionary defines assets in accounting terms and calls them, "The entries on a balance sheet showing all properties, both tangible and intangible and claims against others that may be applied to cover the liabilities of a person or business."

Assets are the entire property owned by a person. It is the kind of goods, money, stock etc. you own which can be used to settle a debt, were you to be bankrupt.

An asset is not just a property you own with a mortgage on it. If you have a property with a mortgage, only the equity of that property may be said to be part of your wealth because the building still carries liability.

Assets can include cash, stock, inventories, property rights and goodwill.

Part of wealth is what is also called fixed assets. These are those that are expected to keep on providing benefits for more than one year such as equipment, buildings, real estate etc.

The net assets are the excess of assets you have over your liabilities. This is possibly the kind of asset by which your true wealth should be measured.

If you count all the number of properties and houses you own and you did not deduct the money of your mortgagors you are missing something. You may consider yourself wealthy when you are not.

## HOW TO BE WEALTHY?

The whole ethos of this book is to communicate the truth that God's wealth is about to be transferred and furthermore the principles by which one can connect to it.

To work though the whole subject of wealth under this title would be to duplicate everything in the whole of the book. However, let me summarise for you some of the steps that lead to wealth creation.

## 1. Wealthy thinking

*For as he thinketh in his heart, so is he: Eat and drink, saith he to thee; but his heart is not with thee. Proverbs 23:7*

This is our first point of reference out of the eight circles. Without a wealthy mind there cannot be a wealthy life. If you desire to have a better life you must make a conscious decision for a transformation of your mind.

A wealthy mind is being conscious and convinced that it is God's desire for you to be blessed.

*Dear friend, I pray that you may enjoy good health and that all may go well with you, even as your soul is getting along well.*
*3 John 2*

This kind of mind is happy by itself before there is a manifestation of the wealth. However, it does not negate, belittle, overlook or dismiss the desires to experience financial increase.

If you do not change the way you think about money you will not be able to hold on to it. If your thoughts are wrong for example you will resent those who are wealthy and you never increase in anything you resent.

## 2. Develop an understanding of the power of small and big savings

When it comes to saving in bits or investing in bits it is a good start. Great armies are built by the recruitment of individual soldiers, one soldier at a time.

## 3. Always spend less than you earn

In the early stages of your wealth creation you may learn to apply the 80/20 principle. Ten per cent of the 20 goes for tithe and the other 10 per cent as a saving; while the 80 per cent is applied to whatever expenses - mortgage, utility bills, transportation etc.

## 4. Always pay yourself first

Once the tithe is deducted, which is the first the next is paying yourself. To handover all your income to creditors would mean that you have not learnt the power of delaying the money in your own investment before paying your creditors.

## 5. Save something out of each dollar

By that action you are buying your own freedom. You see, money has the ability to keep on working even when you are sleeping, eating and resting.

Money has the capacity to become an employee. You can therefore make it your employee which will work hard. You can make a dollar go to the stock exchange and buy share of companies. While you are resting, everyone who goes to trade with that company is influencing your investment in the stocks and shares of such a company.

Minimise the amount of consumer debt you have. There are debts that are for leverage - that you must seek to use. The prophet told the woman to go and borrow vessels.

*Elisha said, "Go around and ask all your neighbors for empty jars. Don't ask for just a few. 2 Kings 4:3*

However, consumer debt - that is using borrowed money for goods and services like furniture, cars etc. would only continue to drain you, sap your energy and keep you working without enjoying the benefits in investment.

## 6. You are responsible for where you are in life

Remember that for wealth creation nobody owes you anything. If you go and spend the money because you could not wait for five, seven or ten years for the yield you will be surprised that the five, seven or ten years you were unwilling to wait for will still come and go.

If you did not invest it comes with nothing and leaves you with nothing.

## 7. Pay cash and use less credit

Every time you use credit i.e. the credit card, you have engaged yourself in spending the money which you have not yet earned and when it is time to pay you pay far in excess of what you have borrowed.

## 8. Buy stocks, not the product

Imagine a company which you patronise often. If you buy the product you will only consume the fruit they produce but if you buy the stocks you will be part-owner of the company.

If your income and wealth continue to go into investments like this you continue to compound all that God has provided for you.

## 9. Keep track of your money

Money should not just come and go with you. Money should not say 'Bye, bye.' You need to form habits that make money attracted to you.

## 10. Study and admire the successful, particularly in your chosen field

Emulate them, appreciate them and associate with them. Who you see determines what you hear, become, achieve, appreciate and respect etc.

## 11. Recognise the difference between income statement wealth and balance sheet wealth

It is not what comes in that makes you wealthy but what you save, invest and compound through interest.

## 12. Do not confuse debt with wealth

If you live in a $2 million dollar home and you still have a $1.5 million dollar mortgage you are not $2 million wealthy, you are $1.5 million in debt.

Really wealthy people work hard to avoid debt.

## 13. Invest

Invest daily, regularly and systematically.

## 14. Form new habits which encourage you in the direction of becoming wealthy for God

When you were born you imbibed certain habits from your parents. Even when money begins to come you will have to understand that money will only magnify those habits that are in you.

## 15. Set financial goals and assess them

It is interesting that while people set goals yearly for themselves they tend to miss out on the need for setting financial goals.

How much do you earn presently? How much do you intend to earn in a year's time? How much are you worth asset wise now? How much do you hope to see your assets grow to in a year's time?

A goal undeclared is a destination unreached.

## 16. Refuse to be stressed

Once you have prayerfully considered and desired to become wealthy and to use it in God's service you must realise that through God you have decided to take control of your financial life from it being run by every challenge you go through.

From then on, do not surrender to other suppositions that go through your mind and all the 'what ifs' that you are likely to be confronted with.

## 17. Make a conscious decision to handle your money matters yourself

This is absolutely important. No one else has an investment in your personal life like you do. We have earlier said, you must surround yourself with champions who are to be your financial mentors.

However, the greatest onus for your financial well-being rests on you.

## 18. Create your own entity

Your own entity gives you the opportunity to increase the volume of your production. It helps you to increase the space - that is the distribution capacity of your company.

Your entity will help you in managing the wealth so that it is not washed away either by statutory outgoings like income tax or by wastages and liabilities.

## 19. Become financially literate

Every available opportunity must be seized to attend a financial seminar. Go to book stands and pick up books so that you are not ignorant of financial matters.

## 20. Give generously

Remember, that is a major part of your life. We shall treat this further as we look at the last circle of wealth creation.

## CIRCLE 6:

# REINVESTMENT

Albert Einstein had said, "The eight wonder of the world is the compounding power of money."

This succinct quote from the physicist basically means that the secret to building wealth is investing in the kind of assets that will create more assets which will result in the investment of those assets in order to create more assets, thus you begin a powerful circle of wealth creation.

A circle of turning income into assets and assets into income continuously is maybe the best way of building the wealth that is sustainable as assets begin to increase and profits from companies swell.

Some people have panicked and their money fears have taken over. Every one of us has a money fear. Some have the fear, when they come out of poverty, that they might one day go back there. Because they dread that journey, they lock up all they have and never even try to reinvest, fearing the loss of everything.

Reinvestment is the key if wealth will be created, increased and built for the use of the service of God.

What do I reinvest, you might ask?

**1.** Profits of the previous businesses, projects, business assignments etc.

**2.** Passive equity - many people are sitting on great wealth, their properties having appreciated and yet do not know what to do.

**3.** Income from assets - how? Imagine a person who is sitting on the equity from an asset. Say, a building which was bought for $50,000 to $100,000 ten years ago, if that property was in an area where the demography has changed and there has been an increase in population, demand for housing would have increased; therefore the value of the property has gone up.

There are many who today are sitting on passive equity, money that has naturally been generated by their real estate but has not been set free to work for the owners.

Reinvestment may mean getting some of that equity in order to invest. This could be done by using the very equity drawn by the building to buy some more buildings. This constitutes more assets, particularly if you buy the kind of buildings which immediately also generate income.

The best possible ones in this regard would be rented apartments. What you have done is to generate income from the buildings bought with the equity from a previous building. The number of your properties increase and the amount generated continues.

As long as reinvestment is done persistently, wealth perpetuation magnifies. With the equity drawn from properties you can get involved in investments directly or indirectly by putting the money in other people's projects. There are those who serve as investors, providing the financing for other people's projects. They share in the profits and while they do this, then ensure that their own money which is the capital for such a project is secured. In the end, the borrower does all the work for them while they share the profit with the borrower. After all they took a risk by putting their money down.

Reinvestment will require that you learn to enjoy it and show interest in doing it. If you must make tangible impact and create the result we are talking about, you will need to make time and be available if it is a direct investment to be able to follow through and see that nothing is left uncovered and the investment is unexposed.

Reinvestment may mean learning to set up more entities to protect even the passive income that is generated from another company. We gave the illustration earlier of the man who takes the equity from his house to buy a rented apartment. If he buys the rented apartment in his name, he has only increased his own tax burden. However, if the equity was drawn and put in a company, the same company can buy these properties, rent them out and only pay company tax.

If the man in question were to live in the United Kingdom, the rented apartment bought in his name may attract 40 to 50 per cent tax if he has already exceeded the lower level of income before taxation. Whereas if the same properties were in the name of a company, the maximum he will pay is 20 per cent tax and that would be after other incentives have been enjoyed by the owner of the company.

What we are saying in effect is that the creation of such a company where you direct the profits from previous investments could help to maximise your money and limit the tax you pay.

In your process of investment you need to surround yourself with other people who know their onions - accountants, lawyers, specialists, marketers and consultants - practically everyone who can help you. As you get them onboard, carry them along in all of your plans because one good idea you have may cost you a lot of money if someone did not show you the weakness of what you want to carry out.

Reinvestment is an assumption that whatever you have is growing at a higher proportion. Once wealth creation reaches this level it becomes necessary for you to involve others; not only to involve them but to rather loose yourself or detach from some of the processes if others can do it better and faster while you focus on what you know to do best.

# CIRCLE 7:
# MULTI-GENERATIONAL WEALTH

One of the characteristics of the truly wealthy is that they do things generationally, laying the foundation for their children, grand and great grandchildren to perpetuate the great cause they have started.

While writing this section of the book, I observed that today, 12th May 2006, the money section of USA Today newspaper carries the story of the CEO and Chairman of Ford Motors, Bill Ford. Over 100 years on and the dreams of a mechanic who started a motor company continue to be perpetuated.

Whatever wealth you have been used of God to generate, it is very important to prepare the next generation to handle it. It is important to discuss with them your intentions before your passage to eternity. Too often, there is very little communicated to those who benefit from such wealth. People were left tremendous wealth and they did not know what mechanisms were put in place which led to such wealth.

How many young people have been messed up by the wealth of their parents who kept mute? How many wealthy people also have failed to teach their heirs how to perpetuate wealth, use money or spend it?

Succession planning is beginning to be a very major discussion in every institution. So it is in the world of wealth. It is very crucial because of the physical, financial and emotional consequence. It may be hard on some of your heirs, but clarifying why you are leaving what for who may mean that there is no fight after you have gone.

For example if a business was involved, you need to determine if you are selling the business and putting the money in trust, handing the money over or keeping the business for them to run. However, always remember business management, particularly on a large scale which creates wealth requires a certain skill. It takes more than a university degree in business administration.

Some heirs have inherited businesses and have taken them from good to great while others have completely destroyed it.

To be able to do this effectively you may require an assessment of the character, ability and needs of your family and each of them. Where you have a spouse, you need to clarify what is to be left for her and how it may be left.

Is she your primary beneficiary? From all indications what is her life expectancy? Will she need support, and if so for how long? Does she have the ability to manage the business? If properties are left, would they need to be sold, the money put in trusts so she can live on what she derives from the trust or can she manage the property or properties?

## EDUCATION

Educating the generation to come in order to continue to perpetuate the wealth you have had to live is two sided. First there is the secular education and there is financial education.

You must ascertain presently what your children's educational status is and if they have not finished, ensuring that you have applied enough funds towards the completion of their studies.

You must also ensure that the one who needs special education has had such requirements attended to.

## FINANCIAL EDUCATION

It is important to have the future generation build financial knowledge and expertise, teaching them how to read a financial statement from when they were young, to understand financial perspectives, bearing in mind that their educational system does not offer any form of financial education and programme.

Therefore the responsibility of developing financial knowledge in your children rests on you. If you want to know how important that is, just imagine how wonderful it would have been if you were actually taught the art and science of wealth management. Not just earning money, but generating and managing wealth. Start such teaching young where possible. The tragedy of today's teenagers is that they know the price of everything and the value of little.

Value can be taught as you teach them the importance of wealth management.

## GIVING

Teach them to give to the philanthropic. Teach them the importance of sowing in the house of God. You can achieve this by discussing your own giving decisions and your reasons for them in order for your children to learn. If you have a young family, prepare your children every Sunday with an offering to give to the Lord.

As you take them along to church, always ensure that they give in the house of God. As your children grow show them the need to establish or possibly open a charitable account for giving purposes only. From such accounts teach them to give to the house of God but also to good causes so that they begin to see from early that they are part of the solution to the challenges in today's world.

Teaching your children the importance of giving helps them to capture the whole essence of the Christian act of serving the Lord with the wealth perpetuated. Remember that this book is about a wealth that is coming to the hands of believers. It is important that when it comes, it be not corrupted by a total diversion of it only to meet our physical and social needs without taking on our Christian responsibility.

## EMPOWER AND PROTECT

Creating multi-generational wealth is empowering. However, such wealth must also be protected. This protection should include ascertaining if properties will be left outright or in trust. If in trust, you should also be sure that the age of the children is clear before they can draw on the principal derived from the trust.

Many have left wealth for their children but did not sort out the tax problem. Some of the wisest and wealthiest have lost tremendous money because they did not look at this area.

J P Morgan built the family fortunes he had into a colossal industry and empire, forming the US Steel Corporation, yet he lost 69 per cent totalling $12 million at that time to taxes and costs at his death because a tax effective system was not put in place.

You must ask yourself, "Am I using available tax shelter opportunities to reduce the combined family income during my life and after my death; am I using available tax shelter opportunities to reduce estate and in-taxes." Do you know how much the estate taxes and administration costs will be on your will? Have you asked experts to check on these? Remember we said it is important to surround yourself with mentors and one of them will be an estate planner who can plan your estate way before you are dead and after you have gone things should be properly done.

John Rockefeller Sr., Frederick Vandervelt, William Boyn all lost almost 50 per cent of their family's wealth to estate taxes and costs.

Would you need to consider transferring properties in your lifetime to your children in order to reduce the size of taxable estate? Will you need to put all your properties in a company and then possibly retire early, making such children directors of the company and in that way, there is no inheritance tax since they are still company properties when you have retired?

## THE WILL

One of the most important instruments of protection of children and spouse in the perpetuation of multi-generational wealth is the will. Do you have a will? When was it executed? When last did you review it with your lawyer? Did you consider using a competent lawyer who knows more about wills or did you get a friend who read something up?

The more the wealth you have generated the more it becomes necessary that you do not buy one of the off-the-shelf wills to use in protecting what God has blessed you with.

In the course of changes in your business, have you carried this on board and adjusted your will accordingly. If it is a trust, have you adjusted the provisions? Have you made an inventory of the properties you own and integrated the transfer of these properties with the will or trust so that your objective of multi-generational wealth is achieved? Have you considered a common disaster clause in your will or trust so that were you and your spouse and/or some of the children involved in a tragedy or a disaster, somebody is still empowered to perpetuate multi-generational wealth? Have you ensured that adopted children and/or descendants or extended family members should inherit certain properties or as natural born children? This is very important so that natural born children do not think adopted ones have no right. Once you have established this, adopted children could be part of the perpetuation of your wealth.

Lastly do not make the mistake of thinking that because your children are all equals the distribution of the wealth should be. There can be equal treatment but equal does not always mean equitable. In other words, not everyone is competent to handle things at the same level as the others. To leave the control of the family business generally in the hands of older children may spell disaster in the future. One of the control mechanisms to put in place may be to give the power and control of decision-making into the hands of the most qualified heir while the value, the worth of the business and that which is derived is shared equally.

## CIRCLE 8:

# GIVING

## A. GIVING TO THE MINISTRY[8]

G iving does not sit well with the nature of man; generally humans would prefer to keep everything they get. In the words of John Avanzini, people would prefer to "Get all they can, can all they get and sit on the can."

*There is that scattereth, and yet increaseth; and there is that withholdeth more than is meet, but it tendeth to poverty. The*

8 Matthew Ashimolowo, The 10Ms of Money, MAMM, London, 2004,pgs.151-184

*liberal soul shall be made fat: and he that watereth shall be
watered also himself. Proverbs 11:24-25*

One needs to understand that God blesses us so we can
provide for the needs of our family, enjoy our life on
earth, but also to be a blessing to others. He wants us to
be a conduit, a pipeline through which He can reach
people who are thirsty, broken and in need of being wet
with the blessing of God.

*For I will pour water upon him that is thirsty, and floods upon
the dry ground: I will pour my spirit upon thy seed, and my
blessing upon thine offspring: Isaiah 44:3*

*When the poor and needy seek water, and there is none, and their
tongue faileth for thirst, I the LORD will hear them, I the God
of Israel will not forsake them. I will open rivers in high places,
and fountains in the midst of the valleys: I will make the
wilderness a pool of water, and the dry land springs of water.
Isaiah 41:17-18*

We are not meant to be mere reservoirs that hold on to
the blessing, but those who will pass it for others too to
enjoy. When God called Abraham, He said He would
bless him to be a blessing to his generation.

The word blessing in Genesis 12:2 does not stand for
increment alone, it also means empowerment.

*And I will make of thee a great nation, and I will bless thee, and
make thy name great; and thou shalt be a blessing: Genesis 12:2*
In effect it means being empowered to empower others.
God said, I will bless you, and you will be a blessing to
others. One of the true tests of maturity in the Christian

faith is your ability to walk away from what you have, as you use it in blessing other people. It is the evidence that you have received the giving nature of God, because God is a giver. Our ability to release what is in our hand, reveals the nature of our Father, who Himself is a giver.

*He that spared not his own Son, but delivered him up for us all, how shall he not with him also freely give us all things?*
*Romans 8:32*

## Why Give?

The whole of Christianity itself was born in the womb of reaching out and giving and therefore the act of giving expresses that great dimension of the Christian faith.

*For God so loved the world, that he gave his only begotten Son, that whosoever believeth in him should not perish, but have everlasting life. John 3:16*

The process of giving and receiving is what makes the cycle of life be perpetuated and be enjoyable. Those who keep it to themselves do not increase. As much as seedless grapes are enjoyable to eat and nutritious to the body, their inability to reproduce themselves means that they end with one generation and with one usage.

When the body is given food, not only does the body give out energy for life, it also releases the wastage. So in effect the body received and the body gave. When the body fails to give out wastage, what was enjoyed in eating becomes a painful experience in the inability to release the waste. We need to understand why we must give, because once the understanding is appreciated, once we come into a revelation of the power of giving, the action become imperative.

We need to give because in all of God's dealings with us, His chief desire, even in our giving, is for our benefit, our own good, and whatever He provides will promote joy in our lives. God wants us to give because His instruction concerning giving is meant to bring blessings to us.

*Give, and it shall be given unto you; good measure, pressed down, shaken together, and running over, shall men give into your bosom. For with the same measure that ye mete withal it shall be measured to you again. Luke 6:38*

Giving increases our credit account with God.

*Not because I desire a gift: but I desire fruit that may abound to your account Philippians 4:17*

God motivates us to give because of the profit which He knows will come into our lives as we walk in obedience.

*If they obey and serve him, they shall spend their days in prosperity, and their years in pleasures. Job 36:11*

*If ye be willing and obedient, ye shall eat the good of the land: Isaiah 1:19*

God gave us His Son because He loved us. We give to people because we love them. We must continue to give because it is an expression of love.

Giving is a mark of maturity and the quality of your giving is a sign of how more like God you are becoming .

*If ye then, being evil, know how to give good gifts unto your children, how much more shall your Father which is in heaven give good things to them that ask him? Matthew 7:11*

Giving is a mark of our detachment from earthly possessions and our attachment to the person of God.

Giving serves as a bridge that connects us to other people's blessing.

*And I will make of thee a great nation, and I will bless thee, and make thy name great; and thou shalt be a blessing: Genesis 12:2*

As we respond in giving our covenant, God establishes the fact that not only will He bless us but also He empowers us to be a blessing.

*Now the LORD had said unto Abram, Get thee out of thy country, and from thy kindred, and from thy father's house, unto a land that I will shew thee: And I will make of thee a great nation, and I will bless thee, and make thy name great; and thou shalt be a blessing: And I will bless them that bless thee, and curse him that curseth thee: and in thee shall all families of the earth be blessed. Genesis 12:1-3*

Giving is necessary because it helps the believer to establish the purpose of God on earth, and that purpose can only be carried out through the preaching of the Word, and the Word can only go forth if a preacher has been sent.

*How then shall they call on him in whom they have not believed? and how shall they believe in him of whom they have not heard? and how shall they hear without a preacher? And how shall they preach, except they be sent? as it is written, How beautiful are the*

*feet of them that preach the gospel of peace, and bring glad tidings*
*of good things! But they have not all obeyed the gospel. For*
*Esaias saith, Lord, who hath believed our report? So then faith*
*cometh by hearing, and hearing by the word of God.*
*Romans 10:14-17*

Believers need to give because it helps to reach the lost.
Those who are committed to the spreading of the Gospel
must recognise that this great cause would only be
possible from the giving of the believers. Giving is
necessary because it is what establishes financial blessing
in the life of a Christian. The force of financial blessing
is released as we give our money.

*But this I say, He which soweth sparingly shall reap also sparing-*
*ly; and he which soweth bountifully shall reap also bountifully.*
*2 Corinthians 9:6*

Giving is the planting of a financial seed in order to
experience a financial harvest.

It is impossible to reap a harvest of the seed you have not
sown. The farmer who complains and limits the seed he
sows or plants has also limited the harvest he will have.
In the same vein the farmer who plants a bountiful seed
has a right to expect a bountiful harvest.

*Be not deceived; God is not mocked: for whatsoever a man soweth,*
*that shall he also reap. Galatians 6:7*

Your level of harvest cannot be divorced from your level
of giving.

*Give, and it shall be given unto you; good measure, pressed down,*
*and shaken together, and running over, shall men give into your*

*bosom. For with the same measure that ye mete withal it shall be measured to you again. Luke 6:38*

God has put in place an inviolable law that seed must produce after its own kind.

*And God said, Let the earth bring forth grass, the herb yielding seed, and the fruit tree yielding fruit after his kind, whose seed is in itself, upon the earth: and it was so. And the earth brought forth grass, and herb yielding seed after his kind, and the tree yielding fruit, whose seed was in itself, after his kind: and God saw that it was good. Genesis 1:11-12*

God has put in place an inviolable law that seedtime and harvest time would not cease.

*While the earth remaineth, seedtime and harvest, and cold and heat, and summer and winter, and day and night shall not cease. Genesis 8:22*

Our giving is one of the highest forms of sacrificial worship. So when we give we are participating in the process of creating a financial future.

*While the earth remaineth, seedtime and harvest, and cold and heat, and summer and winter, and day and night shall not cease. Genesis 8:22*

Giving is a principle of prosperity in contradiction to secular opinions, but which provokes the blessing of the Lord.

*There is that scattereth, and yet increaseth; and there is that withholdeth more than is meet, but it tendeth to poverty. The liberal soul shall be made fat: and he that watereth shall be watered also himself. Proverbs 11:24-25*

In effect it means, that while many think that it is by hoarding that you increase, the Bible says releasing is what brings increase.

Giving honours God as the Lord of all.

*Wherefore David blessed the LORD before all the congregation: and David said, Blessed be thou, LORD God of Israel our father, for ever and ever. Thine, O LORD, is the greatness, and the power, and the glory, and the victory, and the majesty: for all that is in the heaven and in the earth is thine; thine is the kingdom, O LORD, and thou art exalted as head above all. Both riches and honour come of thee, and thou reignest over all; and in thine hand is power and might; and in thine hand it is to make great, and to give strength unto all. Now therefore, our God, we thank thee, and praise thy glorious name. But who am I, and what is my people, that we should be able to offer so willingly after this sort? for all things come of thee, and of thine own have we given thee. O LORD our God, all this store that we have prepared to build thee an house for thine holy name cometh of thine hand, and is all thine own. 1 Chronicles 29:10-14, 16*

Giving is an instrument for the establishment of the covenant between you and God.

The Lord Jesus said, "It is more blessed to give than to receive." Possibly because it is a sign of maturity to be able to give away. One of the most powerful tools for the warfare of life is giving. It opens the windows of heaven, it rebukes every financial devourer, and it stops them dead in their tracks. Giving becomes your powerful seed for a future of a great harvest. It is not an act that is carried out flippantly, but must be thought through and prayerfully approached.

It is the most powerful principle of God designed to be a blessing to both the giver and the recipient. The natural mind may not understand it - it cannot see how letting go will lead to receiving abundance. However, God's Word stands that it is the one who scatters that increases. The unscriptural mind thinks hoarding is the answer and that giving away what you have decreases your net worth, but yet God says it is in that act of giving that we increase.

## What Should We Give?

### 1. Freewill offering

This is called the freewill offering because it involves the action of your will. In other words you are involved in determining the amount to be given.

*Therefore if thou bring thy gift to the altar, and there rememberest that thy brother hath ought against thee; Matthew 5:23*

The wilderness church, which is Israel while travelling to Canaan land, was taught never to appear before the Lord empty handed.

*Three times in a year shall all thy males appear before the LORD thy God in the place which he shall choose; in the feast of Unleavened bread, and in the feast of weeks, and in the feast of tabernacles: and they shall not appear before the LORD empty: Every man shall give as he is able, according to the blessing of the LORD thy God which he hath given thee.*
*Deuteronomy 16:16-17*

This is a principle of kingdoms. We are called kings and our God is the King of kings. In Bible times as well as in ancient lands where kings reigned, a lesser king never appeared before a greater king empty handed. This is a principle also for the kingdom of God. He is the King of kings and we are kings. To appear before Him without an offering is to not fully understand who we are and how to appear before this King of kings. When the Queen of Sheba came before Solomon, she came with gifts. However there is a principle that establishes that when you come with gifts, you should not go empty-handed. On receiving the lesser king's gift, the greater king must bless the lesser king with a more valuable gift.

*And king Solomon gave unto the queen of Sheba all her desire, whatsoever she asked, beside that which Solomon gave her of his royal bounty. So she turned and went to her own country, she and her servants. 1 Kings 10:13*

The freewill offering is what you bring to God to appreciate His good hand on our life and His favour that has been manifesting in the things you do.

Freewill offerings are what you bring to establish fellowship with God.

The freewill offering is what determines the inflow of blessings after the tithe has opened the windows.

The offering establishes fellowship with the King of kings, it is freewill and one is not called to do more than he can, however, there are times when it must be a sacrifice, because the Kingdom of God requires it.

*Take ye from among you an offering unto the LORD: whosoever is of a willing heart, let him bring it, an offering of the LORD; gold, and silver, and brass. Exodus 35:5*

*And it came to pass after these things, that God did tempt Abraham, and said unto him, Abraham: and he said, Behold, here I am. And he said, Take now thy son, thine only son Isaac, whom thou lovest, and get thee into the land of Moriah; and offer him there for a burnt offering upon one of the mountains which I will tell thee of. Genesis 22:1-2*

*And the king said unto Araunah, Nay; but I will surely buy it of thee at a price: neither will I offer burnt offerings unto the LORD my God of that which doth cost me nothing. So David bought the threshingfloor and the oxen for fifty shekels of silver. 2 Samuel 24:24*

God laid claim to Isaac and Abraham knew he had no other choice but to lay him on the altar. He laid Isaac on the altar knowing that whatever followed would be a hundred fold return, like Jesus also taught.

*And every one that hath forsaken houses, or brethren, or sisters, or father, or mother, or wife, or children, or lands, for my name's sake, shall receive an hundredfold, and shall inherit everlasting life. Matthew 19:29*

However when we worship God with our offering, we negate the power of the seed sown when we complain or act as if God owes us and must return quickly what was proportionate to the seed we had sown. God will certainly bless the believer, but it is an offering of worship, and it must truly die at the altar.

## Giving to the Poor

In another chapter we will be talking extensively about the poor, however, the scriptures teach us to give to the poor. We give to the poor to continue our act of benevolence and to be a blessing to others as taught by scriptures.

*So I took the chief of your tribes, wise men, and known, and made them heads over you, captains over thousands, and captains over hundreds, and captains over fifties, and captains over tens, and officers among your tribes. Deuteronomy 1:15*

Scriptures are very clear; you either fall under the category of a person in need of supply or a supplier of the needs.

*He that hath pity upon the poor lendeth unto the LORD; and that which he hath given will he pay him again. Proverbs 19:17*

This passage which we have read supports the statement of the Lord Jesus Christ when He said, "When we give a cup of water to one of the poor, we have done it as to the Lord." When we release what God has provided for us we bring healing to the hurting and become an extension of the kingdom of God.

Giving to the poor becomes an instrument of deliverance from every yoke and danger.

*Blessed is he that considereth the poor: the LORD will deliver him in time of trouble. The LORD will preserve him, and keep him alive; and he shall be blessed upon the earth: and thou wilt not deliver him unto the will of his enemies. Psalm 41:1-2*

The plan of the enemy is the destruction of the poor, but such a plan is foiled because you have chosen to be an instrument of blessing to the poor. David is an example of a man who gave to the poor. When Ziklag was invaded and his family, property and that of his soldiers was carried away by an invading army, David's ability to provide for a hungry Egyptian by the roadside was instrumental to the discovery of what was stolen from him.

When you give to the poor it is not necessarily in order that the anointing upon the poor will release any blessing or favour upon you. But certainly the liberality of your soul provokes the grace of God to cause an increase in your life.

> *There is that scattereth, and yet increaseth; and there is that withholdeth more than is meet, but it tendeth to poverty. The liberal soul shall be made fat: and he that watereth shall be watered also himself. Proverbs 11:24-25*

When the increase comes by reason of blessing the poor, it is also not for you to hoard, but to be able to use in touching more lives.

## 2. The vow or pledge

A vow is a pledge, a commitment made by you to serve the Lord with a special offering, either prior to or after a breakthrough.

A vow often would be what you have chosen before the Lord to do in response to a call to carry out a project or because of a vision you have on your heart. Once a vow is made before the Lord it is binding upon the person who made the vow.

*Thy vows are upon me, O God: I will render praises unto thee.*
*Psalm 56:12*

A vow is a covenant which we have made to the Lord and God therefore holds us responsible for the words we have spoken.

God is good and the level of His goodness is determined by how good His Word is. And because He is good, He expects us to be good with our words.

Our vows reveal our commitment to our worship of God.

*Vow, and pay unto the LORD your God: let all that be round about him bring presents unto him that ought to be feared.*
*Psalm 76:11*

It is a form of worship we have chosen ourselves and therefore the fulfillment becomes important.

*It is a snare to the man who devoureth that which is holy, and after vows to make enquiry. Proverbs 20:25*

It is important to learn that a commitment has been made once you have made a vow. It would have been better if it were not made, so having made it, fulfillment becomes necessary.

*When thou vowest a vow unto God, defer not to pay it; for he hath no pleasure in fools: pay that which thou hast vowed. Better is it that thou shouldest not vow, than that thou shouldest vow and not pay. Ecclesiastes 5:4-5*

Once the vow is made and the believer makes the commitment, God also is committed to you to answer whatever prayer or decree you put forth before Him; He is committed to making them happen.

*Thou shalt make thy prayer unto him, and he shall hear thee, and thou shalt pay thy vows. Thou shalt also decree a thing, and it shall Be established unto thee: and the light shall shine upon thy ways. Job 22:27-28*

Remember the vow is sometimes used as a method of advancing the kingdom of God as we make pledges towards projects.

## How To Fulfil The Stewardship of Giving

God wants us to continue to worship Him with that which He has provided in our giving and not only should we continue but we should increase our levels of giving. However, it must be done with the right spirit and in the right way. It must be done with love. For it to be without love, giving becomes legalism.

*And though I bestow all my goods to feed the poor, and though I give my body to be burned, and have not charity, it profiteth me nothing. 1 Corinthians 13:3*

It must be motivated by our desire to please Him and to be a blessing to other people.

*And the king said unto Araunah, Nay; but I will surely buy it of thee at a price: neither will I offer burnt offerings unto the LORD my God of that which doth cost me nothing. So David bought the threshingfloor and the oxen for fifty shekels of silver. 2 Samuel 24:24*

*And walk in love, as Christ also hath loved us, and hath given himself for us an offering and a sacrifice to God for a sweetsmelling savour. Ephesians 5:2*

It is not the level of giving alone that is important; it is the attitude of the giver that is paramount.

*Honour the LORD with thy substance, and with the firstfruits of all thine increase: Proverbs 3:9*

This in effect means that our offerings stay on earth while our attitude is what God receives. That is why therefore the scriptures teach us not to give grudgingly (2 Corinthians 9:7); out of compulsion (2 Corinthians 9:7); but cheerfully (2 Corinthians 9:7); generously (2 Corinthians 9:5); bountifully (2 Corinthians 9:6); purposefully (2 Corinthians 9:7); abundantly (2 Corinthians 9:8); liberally (2 Corinthians 9:11,13).

*But this I say, He which soweth sparingly shall reap also sparingly; and he which soweth bountifully shall reap also bountifully. Every man according as he purposeth in his heart, so let him give; not grudgingly, or of necessity: for God loveth a cheerful giver. And God is able to make all grace abound toward you; that ye, always having all sufficiency in all things, may abound to every good work: 2 Corinthians 9:6-8*

*Being enriched in every thing to all bountifulness, which causeth through us thanksgiving to God. Whiles by the experiment of this ministration they glorify God for your professed subjection unto the gospel of Christ, and for your liberal distribution unto them, and unto all men; 2 Corinthians 9:11,13*

When giving is done outside of a heart of love, generosity and cheerfulness, the purpose is defeated and the blessing is hindered.

Giving should be planned.

*Upon the first day of the week let every one of you lay by him in store, as God hath prospered him, that there be no gatherings when I come. 1 Corinthians 16:2*

Paul in writing to the Corinthians said they should gather all that they were going to give before he came. This means in effect that the haphazard giving of believers, whereby it is as if they were caught unawares on Sunday morning, also reflects what they should expect in the realm of the spirit. So nothing precludes you from praying every January on what your level of offering should be each year, or to pray before you go to a meeting as to what you should give to the Lord.

Recognise also that the quality and quantity of your seed determines the quality and quantity of your harvest. Bear in mind that once you set the percentage or level of giving, you have already fixed the level of blessing that will flow to you. Sowing generously produces reaping generously.

*Give, and it shall be given unto you; good measure, pressed down, and shaken together, and running over, shall men give into your bosom. For with the same measure that ye mete withal it shall be measured to you again. Luke 6:38*

In the same vein the person who sows sparingly will have produced back to him a sparing or limited harvest.

Give under all circumstances; do not wait until it is comfortable and convenient to give. The person who has learnt to give in times of challenges and has been consistent with giving will experience the continuous supply of God. Giving to the Lord must always be with a heart that responds to whatever the Lord tells you to do. For example, God fixed the tithe and obedience to it must be 100 per cent.

Certainly God never wants a person to go beyond their ability in the giving of their offering. It is no use giving and jeopardising the happiness of the giver, but make sure that you never come before the Lord empty handed. You cannot replace the act of giving with fasting, praying or prophesying. Though they are good Christian actions they do not replace the act of covenant that is expressed in giving.

*Every man according as he purposeth in his heart, so let him give;*
*not grudgingly, or of necessity: for God loveth a cheerful giver.*
*2 Corinthians 9:7*

It should not be done haphazardly as we said earlier on, but rather as a person investing in the Kingdom of heaven. When the tabernacle of God was to be built in the wilderness, Moses knew the people had the gold, yet he asked that whatever giving was to be done must be done willingly.

*Take ye from among you an offering unto the LORD: whosoever*
*is of a willing heart, let him bring it, an offering of the LORD;*
*gold, and silver, and brass, Exodus 35:5*

Never give in the atmosphere of grudge or force, rather with excitement in order to know the blessings that would follow. That also helps you so that if there were a delay in the manifestation of your blessing, it does not stop your ability to celebrate the goodness of God.

Never give out of a corrupt heart; if there is a sin problem, ensure that you have repented and moved on.

*And when ye stand praying, forgive, if ye have ought against any: that your Father also which is in heaven may forgive you your trespasses. Mark 11:25*

Never give an offering that will make your family go through financial difficulties or cause anyone to grumble.

The act of obedience must be matched by the act of recognising the importance of you rejoicing in the step you have taken.

## Why People Do Not Give

People do not give because of their lack of knowledge.

If you are ignorant of what God said concerning giving, you will hold back because your nature says to do so. People do not give because of their ignorance of their covenant rights and blessings that follows giving by the believer. People do not give because of their lack of understanding of the responsibility of the believer in being part of the perpetuation of the Gospel.

*How then shall they call on him in whom they have not believed? and how shall they believe in him of whom they have not heard? and how shall they hear without a preacher? And how shall they preach, except they be sent? as it is written, How beautiful are the feet of them that preach the gospel of peace, and bring glad tidings of good things! But they have not all obeyed the gospel. For Esaias saith, Lord, who hath believed our report? So then faith*

*cometh by hearing, and hearing by the word of God.*
*Romans 10:14-17*

Some other people do not give because they express fear. They are afraid that God might not do what He promised.

*For all the promises of God in him are yea, and in him Amen, unto the glory of God by us. 2 Corinthians 1:20*

Some are afraid that as they tithe or release their offering it might not work for their increase; however God is not a man that He should lie.

*God is not a man, that he should lie; neither the son of man, that he should repent: hath he said, and shall he not do it? or hath he spoken, and shall he not make it good? Numbers 23:19*

Fear also makes people want to give from what they control, unknown to them that it is not until they release it that they can know how God can increase it. Some others are afraid because they look at the mitigating circumstances, the situations in which they are, and refuse to give.

*He that observeth the wind shall not sow; and he that regardeth the clouds shall not reap. As thou knowest not what is the way of the spirit, nor how the bones do grow in the womb of her that is with child: even so thou knowest not the works of God who maketh all. In the morning sow thy seed, and in the evening withhold not thine hand: for thou knowest not whether shall prosper, either this or that, or whether they both shall be alike good. Ecclesiastes 11:4-6*

Selfishness is a major reason why many stop short of

giving or worshipping God with their tithes and offering. The innate nature of man says, "Keep it to yourself, why release it?" The innate nature of man says, "Do it yourself." However that ends up in closing the windows of heaven, and the worse thing is to try and operate under a closed heaven. The innate nature of man, the selfish nature of man causes people to miss a major opportunity to act like Jesus and be givers. He was the Ultimate Giver.

However, if anything has been major in stopping people from giving towards the kingdom it is deception that is brought by the culture around us. This culture would say that preachers are the ones grabbing our money and therefore we should keep it to ourselves. This is a knee-jerk reaction and shortsighted because a man has no power to hinder your blessing once the seed from your hand has been released.

There are also religious lies that can hold a person down, lies we tell ourselves like, "the poorer the better". We misconstrue scriptures and say things to the effect that, "Maybe rich men won't go to heaven." We dealt with this under 'The Mindset'.

## The Consequence Of Not Giving

We have established that one of the key reasons God wants us to give is for the establishment and promotion of His Kingdom. The greatest consequence of not giving to God is financial barrenness. This is what we will look at in more detail.

Whenever there is financial barrenness, there is always a missing element that needs to be put in perspective. To lack financially is a challenge, but to be financially barren is even tougher.

Causes of financial barrenness would be:

## 1. The unwillingness primarily to build the Kingdom of God

*Thus speaketh the LORD of hosts, saying, This people say, The time is not come, the time that the LORD'S house should be built. Haggai 1:2*

The people in the book of Haggai had rejoiced at their deliverance from Babylonian captivity and possibly promised a vow to rebuild His temple, but no sooner did they get to the land than they forgot the vows they made.

## 2. The neglect of the things of the Lord

*Is it time for you, O ye, to dwell in your cieled houses, and this house lie waste? Haggai 1:4*

## 3. Preference for one's personal security to the well-being of the ministry and the things of God

*Ye looked for much, and, lo, it came to little; and when ye brought it home, I did blow upon it. Why? saith the LORD of hosts. Because of mine house that is waste, and ye run every man unto his own house. Haggai 1:9*

Jesus told the story of the rich man whose focus was upon himself. He was so selfish that he did not realise why God brings the blessing. The blessing was to touch the world, not just for personal gain. Those who are unable to make Kingdom investments would not know Kingdom enjoyment. Those who do not know Kingdom addiction would not experience supernatural addition. Such people become very busy building an empire for themselves.

The people in the book of Haggai withheld their tithes and all their other givings. When the tithe is withheld the curse is released on whatever is left. When there is a curse on what you have, hard work cannot break the cycle of defeat.

*Ye are cursed with a curse: for ye have robbed me, even this whole nation. Malachi 3:9*

## The consequences of financial barrenness

Solomon said one of the things that is never satisfied is a womb that has never borne a child.

*The horseleach hath two daughters, crying, Give, give. There are three things that are never satisfied, yea, four things say not, It is enough: The grave; and the barren womb; the earth that is not filled with water; and the fire that saith not, It is enough. Proverbs 30:15-16*

When you go through financial barrenness, you work hard and have no fruit to show.

## 1. There will be poor results

*Ye have sown much, and bring in little; ye eat, but ye have not enough; ye drink, but ye are not filled with drink; ye clothe you, but there is none warm; and he that earneth wages earneth wages to put it into a bag with holes. Haggai 1:6*

## 2. Unsatisfied desire

A man under the curse of financial barrenness keeps pursuing and never meets his target. Such a person has a deep hunger but his thirst and hunger is never satisfied. Financial barrenness is a life that is more like chasing a shadow and never meeting up. Financial barrenness brings physical brokenness. Sickness and disease follow disobedience in the act of withholding the tithe and the offering. It follows when financial barrenness is manifested.

## 3. Social degradation

*Ye have sown much, and bring in little; ye eat, but ye have not enough; ye drink, but ye are not filled with drink; ye clothe you, but there is none warm; and he that earneth wages earneth wages to put it into a bag with holes. Haggai 1:6*

When a man walks in disobedience he becomes socially degraded. "They wear clothes but they are never warm." In other words a life of embarrassment and shame becomes the portion of a man who has withheld what he ought to have used to serve the Lord.

Social degradation is the portion of the man that is under the scourge of financial barrenness. So when God said He would deliver His people from shame, a disobedient Christian has just exposed himself to what he should have been delivered from.

## 4. Economic wastage

Unsolicited bills, emergencies that are not planned for, indulgences that cannot be broken from are the things that follow. When monies are withheld from God, particularly the tithe, God will collect it back and that with 20 per cent interest.

One of the ways it is collected back is by the shutting down of things in the life of the disobedient.

## 5. Shattered dreams

God said they would look for much but indeed it would come to    little.   Dreams will not match realities. The hopes of a financially barren person will be shattered, inflation follows, the nation, the people, families who refuse to honour God will find things inflated all around them.   There will be more, but they are only able to buy less.

## 6. Domestic problems

Family arguments, marital problems follow where there is financial barrenness. Eighty-five per cent of family troubles in the modern world are centred around finance. Either the lack of it or in some cases much abundance becomes the reason for family fights.  Where the family has learnt to honour the Lord, the little they have is with the peace of God. Contentment follows the other supplies they have.

## 7. Short-lived victory

If they had any victory at all, the heavens withhold the dew.

*Therefore the heaven over you is stayed from dew, and the earth is stayed from her fruit. Haggai 1:10*

## 8. Perpetual lack

A man is under financial barrenness when heaven withholds its blessings. The man operates under a closed heaven, and to be under a closed heaven means prayers are not answered, and heaven is like brass. Wherever the man who has the heavens closed over him turns, things do not work, rather things are difficult.

Flying over a desert like the Sahara in Africa, all you can see is brown land, because the place has not known rain or moisture in many years. The same effect rests upon the life of a man who is under financial barrenness. This is more than lack; he is barren, not bearing fruit. There is a lot of activity but no fruit.

## 9. Withdrawal of God's approval

*Therefore the heaven over you is stayed from dew, and the earth is stayed from her fruit. Haggai 1:10*

When the approval of heaven is withdrawn from a man, he is like the rebellious that dwell in deserts, who makes his gathering with scorpions and desert foxes.

*God setteth the solitary in families: he bringeth out those which are bound with chains: but the rebellious dwell in a dry land. Psalm 68:6*

## 10. Absence of divine blessing

When heaven withholds its dew, it is symbolic of spiritual dryness. When heaven withholds its blessing, the inner man rots, beautiful things become ugly, businesses collapse, children go wayward, people depend on past glory and repetition. Their lives become deflated; devourers come and break down all that the man has built.

*And I will restore to you the years that the locust hath eaten, the cankerworm, and the caterpiller, and the palmerworm, my great army which I sent among you. Joel 2:25*

Long hours of work do not present evidence of any blessing.

*I returned, and saw under the sun, that the race is not to the swift, nor the battle to the strong, neither yet bread to the wise, nor yet riches to men of understanding, nor yet favour to men of skill; but time and chance happeneth to them all. Ecclesiastes 9:11*

Works that blossomed become represented by mere dust.

## 11. Divine sanctions

*And I called for a drought upon the land, and upon the mountains, and upon the corn, and upon the new wine, and upon the oil, and upon that which the ground bringeth forth, and upon men, and upon cattle, and upon all the labour of the hands. Haggai 1:11*

Consequently everything is withheld and whatever remains has dried up. The rain falls elsewhere but not on the land of the man who is under financial barrenness.

*And also I have withholden the rain from you, when there were yet three months to the harvest: and I caused it to rain upon one city, and caused it not to rain upon another city: one piece was rained upon, and the piece whereupon it rained not withered. So two or three cities wandered unto one city, to drink water; but they were not satisfied: yet have ye not returned unto me, saith the LORD. Amos 4:7-8*

When there is a divine sanction, devourers take over such a life.

*I have smitten you with blasting and mildew: when your gardens and your vineyards and your fig trees and your olive trees increased, the palmerworm devoured them: yet have ye not returned unto me, saith the LORD. Amos 4:9*

Nations of the earth have known sanctions from the United Nations and at such times things are difficult, but imagine when it is a divine sanction. With such upon Israel, their grain was affected; there was no new wine, which is symbolic of joy. No oil, which is symbolic of the anointing. The cattle died, which is symbolic of bad investments and bad returns. The labour of their hands went sour, which meant physical death. Lives became deflated. In like manner those under divine sanctions experience something similar.

Financial barrenness means barely surviving, scanty crops; it makes a person to be struggling, trying to survive when he should have an abundant life.

*Therefore the heaven over you is stayed from dew, and the earth is stayed from her fruit. Haggai 1:10*

*The thief cometh not, but for to steal, and to kill, and to destroy: I am come that they might have life, and that they might have it more abundantly. John 10:10*

## 12. Poor returns and depleted savings

*Is the seed yet in the barn? yea, as yet the vine, and the fig tree, and the pomegranate, and the olive tree, hath not brought forth: from this day will I bless you. Haggai 2:19*

## 13. Economic ruin

*And I called for a drought upon the land, and upon the mountains, and upon the corn, and upon the new wine, and upon the oil, and upon that which the ground bringeth forth, and upon men, and upon cattle, and upon all the labour of the hands. Haggai 1:11*

When favour is withdrawn and heaven is closed, the atmosphere of financial barrenness prevails. God ceases to smile on His people because the tithe is withheld, the offering is not given and His work suffers neglect. Under these circumstances the people refuse to fulfil the vows they made in His presence. Sowing into the life of a man of God does not provoke the anointing on a man of God and the poor are not blessed or helped. Economic ruin becomes inevitable.

## 14. Phantom pregnancy

*Like as a woman with child, that draweth near the time of her delivery, is in pain, and crieth out in her pangs; so have we been in thy sight, O LORD. We have been with child, we have been in pain, we have as it were brought forth wind; we have not wrought any deliverance in the earth; neither have the inhabitants of the world fallen. Isaiah 26:17-18*

The worst consequence of financial barrenness is to carry a dream and give birth to nothing. It is to carry a picture, an idea, or a vision, to work so hard and have no result, no fruit to show for it. The word here for wind also means anger, wrath or temper. In other words when vision is unfulfilled, when dreams do not happen because of disobedience, one becomes quick-tempered, angry at God, man and everything because of the dreams that do not match the reality of life. It also means to be despondent, to be breathless.

## The Cure for Financial Barrenness

*Obviously from this chapter, the cure for financial barrenness is to go back to giving. However before there is a giving, there must be repentance because God deserves to be fully obeyed, not partially. God deserves to be revered, respected, venerated and honoured above all gods. Thus saith the LORD of hosts; Consider your ways. Haggai 1:7*

*Then Zerubbabel the son of Shealtiel, and Joshua the son of Josedech, the high priest, with all the remnant of the people, obeyed the voice of the LORD their God, and the words of Haggai the prophet, as the LORD their God had sent him, and the people did fear before the LORD. Haggai 1:12*

The believer must learn to walk by God's instruction, not by people's opinion. Haggai came back after the seventh month with a word from the Lord, challenging the people that truly there will be change if they learn to serve Him.

The Word of God is with us and in our hands today. As we read it we must obey. The tithe must not be given only in moments of convenience, but one must recognise that it is a command that produces a commanded blessing.

*As the dew of Hermon, and as the dew that descended upon the mountains of Zion: for there the LORD commanded the blessing, even life for evermore. Psalm 133:3*

We must now follow our repentance with an expectant heart. Expectation is necessary for experience.

*Who is left among you that saw this house in her first glory? and how do ye see it now? is it not in your eyes in comparison of it as nothing? Haggai 2:3*

## Be strong

*Yet now be strong, O Zerubbabel, saith the LORD; and be strong, O Joshua, son of Josedech, the high priest; and be strong, all ye people of the land, saith the LORD, and work: for I am with you, saith the LORD of hosts: Haggai 2:4*

Because it has been bad in the past does not mean that it will always be.

## Be led by the Lord

*Yet now be strong, O Zerubbabel, saith the LORD; and be strong, O Joshua, son of Josedech, the high priest; and be strong, all ye people of the land, saith the LORD, and work: for I am with you, saith the LORD of hosts: Haggai 2:4*

Circumstances must not lead the believer when it comes to the stewardship of giving. Neither should what our friends think or say. For many people it is not their friends or circumstances, but their spouse. If you are married to a person who is unsaved you would need to walk in a lot of wisdom when it comes to the bringing of the tithe to the storehouse, and therefore you may have to pray and wait for the right moment. However, if both are believers, they are obliged to serve the Lord with that which He has provided for them, submitting to God as the Lord of all things is necessary to make progress.

## Be bold

*According to the word that I covenanted with you when ye came out of Egypt, so my spirit remaineth among you: fear ye not.*
*Haggai 2:5*

Fear is a thief of the blessing of God. Fear will seize the breath in your spirit and make you panic. It will stop you from maximising and reaching your highest fulfillment in life. Boldness is necessary to be able to release what God has provided for us. Boldness is also necessary for you to go in and take what God has already prepared for you. God wants you to prosper and no devil can stop you.

When you repent and walk in obedience, when you revere God for who He is, the result of course will be:

## 1. Divine visitation

*And I will shake all nations, and the desire of all nations shall come: and I will fill this house with glory, saith the LORD of hosts. Haggai 2:7*

## 2. Glory will be restored back into your finances and every area of your life

*And I will shake all nations, and the desire of all nations shall come: and I will fill this house with glory, saith the LORD of hosts. Haggai 2:7*

Nothing is as tough as a life without glory; nothing is as empty as a life that does not know the glory of the Lord.

*And the glory of the LORD shall be revealed, and all flesh shall see it together: for the mouth of the LORD hath spoken it.*
*Isaiah 40:5*

## 3. Financial breakthrough will follow you

*The silver is mine, and the gold is mine, saith the LORD of hosts. Haggai 2:8*

God says that all silver and gold belong to Him; so do not let the devil talk you out of your blessing. Have no apologies for desiring to be blessed, after all it belongs to your Father and it is His work you want to use it for. Satan owns nothing that is why the scripture calls him a thief.

*The thief cometh not, but for to steal, and to kill, and to destroy:*
*John 10:10*

Whatever he has was stolen from believers who do not know their authority and dominion rights. God made the silver and the gold when He laid the foundation of the earth. We are yet to come into the greatest blessing God has for His people because they are the ones He will use for the propagation of His Word in these last days.

## 4. There will be abundant peace

*The glory of this latter house shall be greater than of the former, saith the LORD of hosts: and in this place will I give peace, saith the LORD of hosts. Haggai 2:9*

Once obedience is put in place, the revelation of the blessing of God will far exceed the troubles you have seen.

It is safe to say whether it is the tithe, offering, vows or blessing the poor, giving is living. God has not left room for questions when it comes to obeying Him either in the tithe or in serving Him with our offering. When He called Abraham, "Get thee out," Abraham did not say, "Where and why am I going?" The Bible says, "So Abraham departed."

When you get excited about obeying God, God will be happy to lift you and promote you beyond imagination.

*Praise ye the LORD. Blessed is the man that feareth the LORD, that delighteth greatly in his commandments. Wealth and riches shall be in his house: and his righteousness endureth for ever.*
*Psalm 112:1,3*

As we serve the Lord with that which He has provided for us, let us do it with a heart of purity.

*O LORD our God, all this store that we have prepared to build thee an house for thine holy name cometh of thine hand, and is all thine own. I know also, my God, that thou triest the heart, and hast pleasure in uprightness. As for me, in the uprightness of mine heart I have willingly offered all these things: and now have I seen with joy thy people, which are present here, to offer willingly unto thee. O LORD God of Abraham, Isaac, and of Israel, our fathers, keep this for ever in the imagination of the thoughts of the heart of thy people, and prepare their heart unto thee:*
*1 Chronicles 29:16-18*

Let us recognise and elevate the lordship of the Lord Jesus Christ in everything we do, so that we will see in our hands a harvest. Enjoy the blessing God is bringing as His favour that flows from Him. He is our Father from whom all blessings flow. Obey God in giving and worship Him with that which He provides.

Every New Year make it a habit to think of starting the year with a new level of giving. That certainly will bring you into a new level of receiving. Be free with your giving, never let giving look like a burden to you. Make it a faith step. Rejoice at the opportunity to serve God with the substance He has provided. Always remember you will never achieve your full potential unless you are free to release what is in your hand. It is when you release what is in your hand that you can receive what is in God's hand.

Obedience is crucial. It cannot be belittled, or put aside. It is only those who are willing and obedient that will eat the best of the land.

*If ye be willing and obedient, ye shall eat the good of the land:*
*Isaiah 1:19*

Intimacy is paramount; it is your acquaintance with God that will bring you into His gold.

*Acquaint now thyself with him, and be at peace: thereby good*
*shall come unto thee. Then shalt thou lay up gold as dust, and the*
*gold of Ophir as the stones of the brooks. Job 22:21, 24*

Covenant blessing and breakthrough is not provoked by chance, but by obedience.[8]

---

8 Matthew Ashimolowo, The 10Ms of Money, MAMM, London, 2004,pgs.151-184

## B. GIVING TO GOOD CAUSES

People who were born between 1945 and 1965 are known in the language of sociology as the baby boomers. These were a post world war generation. Globally they have also been known to be the wealthiest generation. Many of the wealthy people, middle class and lower middle class people we know of fall within this category.

From 2010 they will begin to go into retirement. This in itself will release a lot of wealth into the society as some of them begin to sell the big houses they live in, in order to enjoy the rest of their lives, possibly in smaller apartments.

Some may pass on and therefore have to leave tremendous wealth for their children.

Creating wealth for the future, preparing ourselves to also experience supernatural wealth would mean learning the principle of sowing and reaping.

*"As long as the earth endures, seedtime and harvest, cold and heat, summer and winter, day and night will never cease."*
*Genesis 8:22*

*Do not be deceived: God cannot be mocked. A man reaps what he sows. Galatians 6:7*

This means that a large amount will be left or transferred to the next generation who may not necessarily be prepared to handle such sudden increase in assets.

The eight circles of wealth creation which we have shared must not stay with the person who starts the wealth creation but must also pass on to the children.

Wealth must not be the only thing left, but the values underwriting the use of it. Children are likely to come to the financial table with the attitude that money was made for just spending and/or investing and not see the philanthropic part of it.

John D Rockefeller said, "Never think you need to apologise for asking someone to give to a worthy cause, anymore than as though you were giving him or her an opportunity to participate in a high grade investment. The duty of giving is as much his or her's as is the duty of asking yours."

Andrew Carnegie also said, "He who dies rich dies disgraced."

We must not assume that young people do not want to give. In the words of Susan Price, in her book 'The giving family: Raising our children to help others' she said, "Children are born with natural empathy but parents must nurture young people's desire to do good."

Why would a person want to give away the wealth they have created? What impact has this got on continuing to create wealth.

**1.** The first reason God would entrust you with wealth is because as a believer you have the capacity to do a greater good with it.

*But as for you, ye thought evil against me; but God meant it unto good, to bring to pass, as it is this day, to save much people alive.*
*Genesis 50:20*

**2.** The level of wealth that impacts the community is only entrusted in order for you to be a distribution centre

God said to Abraham, "You will be a blessing."

*I will make you into a great nation and I will bless you; I will make your name great, and you will be a blessing. Genesis 12:2*

**3.** Charitable giving is also motivated by the desire of the wealthy to make a difference.

The John D Rockefeller Foundation, Ford Foundation, the Peabody Trust and millions of others around the world are the efforts of the wealthy to make the world a better place.

**4.** Gratefulness

Benevolence is a picture of your gratefulness for life or the opportunity to touch other people. It is important for children to be taught this so they can see that in giving we are ourselves grateful for the opportunities that life has given us. It may not be easy for them to part with that which they have if we have not taught them from childhood. But with continuous training anything is possible.

> "There are only two things a child will share willingly: communicable diseases and his mother's age." -
> **Modern maturity**

**5.** The prospect of death which leads people to ask how they want to be remembered decides their commitment to giving.

> Just like we quoted earlier, "He who dies rich dies disgraced." - **Andrew Carnegie**

Each one of us will be remembered, either by those close to us or by those who have benefited from the greater good which we have done.

> "If you give money, spend yourself with it." - **Henry David Thoreau**

**6.** Giving as tax incentive

Probably one of the benefits of modern taxation systems is the opportunity for the tax payer to get a reduction in the amount of tax deducted from him as a result of his commitment and generosity to charities, foundations and organizations like the Red Cross, Christian Aid, churches etc.

In the United Kingdom this is taken even further. For every amount of money you commit to charities the Inland Revenue gives a certain percentage to the same charitable organization. However, this is only an incentive given to tax payers.

**7.** The desire to identify with a cause

The world was shaken on Boxing Day of December 2004 when the biggest tsunami on records hit our planet, shaking Asia and causing the death of close to 300,000 people, not to count the financial consequence which ran to billions of dollars.

That tragedy provoked the generosity of mankind in a way that has never been seen. There are many of such tragedies, incidences that have happened around the world and have provoked financial responses from individuals e.g. the Katrina incident in Louisiana.

**8.** The joy of giving

Nothing pleasures one's heart like meeting people whom you have empowered; students whose school fees you paid or families for who you provided shelter.

Our church was privileged to give enough money to build 40 homes for the victims of the tsunami in Sri Lanka. Imagine visiting such homes and meeting people who are now sheltered because of the generosity of one congregation.

Giving breaks you from the general assumption that money was made to maintain a lifestyle and meet your family's needs. It helps you to touch the world for greater good and do much more through sacrifice.

> "If you are outraged at conditions then you can't possibly be free or happy until you devote all your time to changing them and do nothing but that. But you can't change anything if you want to hold on to a good job, a good way of life and avoid sacrifice." -
> **Cesar Chavez**

How can you carry your children along in the process of being givers in the house of God and good causes?

Let us bear in mind here that the primary reason why

God would bless the believer tremendously with great wealth is in order to make ministry his primary goal, his first commitment.

This commitment must be discussed with your children in order for them to learn from your commitment to giving. They must see the need for sacrificing, the need to not live for oneself alone but to be others-centered.

> "I have the audacity to believe that people everywhere can have three meals a day for their bodies, education and culture for their minds, and dignity, quality and freedom for their spirit. I believe that what self-centered men have turn down, other-centered men can build up." - **Martin Luther King**

Teach your children wealth creation through giving.

## How to carry your children along?

I will assume that you are your children's role model. Therefore the best way to teach them about giving will be by example.

Secondly, talk about experiences you have had while volunteering and serving other people. Let them see and know that you have given service in touching other lives in spite of whatever wealth you have.

If you are a worker in the church, let them see your commitment in serving the Lord in the house of God. But even better, when next you are going to serve, take them along, whether it is a soup kitchen or in a major fundraising event.

Make giving an everyday project of your life. Let them see how you have an account from where you give out to meet different needs.

Help your children to make giving decisions: who they want to give to? Why they want to give?

Teach them to recognize that whatever the Lord has blessed them with, their primary commitment is serving the Lord with such wealth and then helping the cause of humanity, the environment and every other challenge around.

# ESTABLISHING YOUR FINANCIAL FUTURE

# VALUES VISION AND VOLUME

**Y**our commitment to go through this book is the indication of a possible desire to experience the wealth transfer which we have taken the time to elaborate in this book.

However if you must appropriate its content and experience the prophecy, it is predicated on the last three things which we share in this chapter.

The establishment of personal financial values, the

clarification of vision and the determination of the volumes you desire.

## 1. YOUR FINANCIAL *VALUES*

We will start with the values you have on the matter of money because it is clear that the vision or goals you set will be based on your personal values.

Values are what we hold dear, what we believe in and would like to represent. If we achieve a vision or goal which is not related to the financial values we hold, the success may not give us gratification. We will probably feel unrewarded and dissatisfied.

Therefore, without knowing what is important to you, you will find it difficult to set satisfying goals and visions.

When you understand what your values are, you will find it easier to achieve your dream.

The establishment of values will also allow you to decide which vision or goal are most important and worth working towards.

Your money values will determine what your financial dislikes, likes, decisions, actions and emotions are.

*Do not love the world or anything in the world. If anyone loves the world, the love of the Father is not in him. For everything in the world-the cravings of sinful man, the lust of his eyes and the boasting of what he has and does-comes not from the Father but from the world. 1 John 2:15-16*

*You adulterous people, don't you know that friendship with the world is hatred toward God? Anyone who chooses to be a friend of the world becomes an enemy of God. James 4:4*

It is not hard to know what a man's financial values are. They are always reflected in what he spends most of his money on.

Essentially, money is neutral, it takes on the character of its owner. Money in the hand of a drug user becomes what that person is. The same money could be exchanged and it finally gets into the hand of a person who will use it for the furtherance of the Gospel.

When used within the context of the sacred community it becomes an expression of values and a commitment to godly actions in the world.

What we are saying in effect is that your money value determines what money means to you. Your money value determines what you do with money. Your money value determines if you have money or if it has you.

When you meet people who overvalue money and treat it like a god, it shows in effect that they have a misplaced value.

One paramount area where our money values goes to show is our attitude when it comes to investing the money God provides.

We have taken quite a bit of time to establish the necessity for investment and reinvestment in order to become a conduit for wealth creation and transfer.

However, this process must not lead to an unethical pursuit of money leaving aside the Christian ethos and values which we hold.

It is only conventional wisdom that says we must abandon ethics when making financial decisions. What people do with their money in the natural world may not mean much; however, in the Christian faith and particularly because it is supposed to be money coming into our hands from God, using the conduits around us, we must also be ready to use it to honour His name and not to be seen promoting that which dishonours the Gospel.

That means in effect that you must be seen to be investing with your values.

This helps you to identify your priorities and it guards you through the process of creating a value-inclusive portfolio which can work for you.

In other words if you approach an investor or someone who is to help you with your investment, you must always ask them if where they intend to put your money is value based.

The believer must not forget that you are God's agent for making His wealth available on earth and therefore there must be a willingness to identify and consider those Christian values which you hold and not somebody else's agenda.

Pursuing wealth creation with values behind your mind means in effect that you want your money to do good.

The other aspect of the values we place on money might not be expressed but is in the inner recess of our hearts. It determines if money comes to us.

Some have a negative attitude to wealth creation, they despise those who seem to be wealthy and affluent and do not realise that what you despise never increases for you. It is a sign that you disrespect it.

Your value system may be an expression that you are unable to handle financial success. The man who was given one talent manifested his money values in the things he said and in the actions he carried out. He went and buried the talent. Jesus said he could have looked for the simplest investment method to compound and increase its value but he did not because his money values did not hold any incremental process as being important.

There are believers who waste the resources they already have, make no effort at increasing it and yet complain daily that they are broke, unknown to them that their actions already reveal their money values.

If your money values are negative they will sabotage your ability to increase it, sabotage your Christianity possibly because you will not be able to do much and in the end hinder your destiny.

What you admire is what you will respect and what you will end up handling. If you have no financial vision and value it will not flow in your direction.

## WHAT ARE FINANCIAL *VALUES*?

Money values include, among all the things we have shared in this book:

- ঙ Using it for service
- ঙ Becoming financially free
- ঙ Experiencing financial security
- ঙ Enjoying financial independence
- ঙ Ensuring respect and appreciation of others

Some would also include the use of it as a success symbol.

## ESTABLISHING FINANCIAL *VALUES*

There is an increase in the avenues which you can use to invest money today.

However, the blind commitment of your funds to some of these investment opportunities may be an indirect promotion of what you are likely to have issues with as a Christian.

Firstly it would be wise for you to only invest after you have screened some of the mutual funds, stocks and bonds that are available to ensure that the monies are not committed in performing the acts or carrying out the businesses which you do not endorse.

Secondly, you may need to engage yourself as an investor or shareholder with the companies that have your funds, encouraging them in community and social responsibility. Unless someone speaks out, most banks, corporations and businesses that handle funds tend to be more profit driven before they think of their social responsibilities.

Thirdly you will need to screen out, question and possibly drop the services of unethical companies. There will always be arguments from the companies investing your funds that profit will be limited; however, this is not so if it is thoughtfully, wisely and carefully applied.

Ethical funds can still make great profits. Moreover you can always let such investment houses know that you intend to marry your financial vision with your values.

## PROPAGATING THE *VALUES*

*Train a child in the way he should go, and when he is old he will not turn from it. The rich rule over the poor, and the borrower is servant to the lender. Proverbs 22:6-7*

Like me, you were probably raised in a home where there was never any teaching on finance. It is interesting that though we wake up and hit the road from nine to five, Monday to Friday, working hard, parents never really take the time to think that they should give their children financial education.

We have already established the need for this; however, we also need to teach our children the place of values in the pursuit of money.

Teach them how to spend responsibly. Help your children to learn how to postpone their gratification and not buy everything they want. Of course, this can be made clear by letting them know there is a difference between what you need and what you want.

Take it further by setting boundaries and limits for your children as they grow up - what they may not have at a certain age. This makes them to begin to place value on money and associate it with maturing.

Earlier on we said, "Teach the children to give." This is a major money value for them to realise that it is not him who amassed a lot but the one who, with the little he has blessed the world.

Teach your children to use their allowances wisely. Show them how to break it into bits. Some to spend, save and thirdly to give away to charity or the church.

Show them how to have their own personal checking account, to pay bills, write cheques and reconcile accounts every month.

Many who have fallen into indebtedness and bad credit are in that condition because at no time did anyone give them a structure for financial management. No one ever taught them how to have personal money values.

The younger ones need a piggy bank so from childhood they can place value on the pennies they get. Move such a child, when he grows older from saving the pennies to opening an account so that they see a graduation.

There is no platform where money is ever taught - that is the reason why these values should be given to them from home.

Where possible allow your children to participate in the family's money making and spending decisions. This will energise their mind and help them prepare for later life.

## 2.    YOUR FINANCIAL *VISION*

*Where there is no revelation, the people cast off restraint; but*
*blessed is he who keeps the law. Proverbs 29:18*

There has been a lot of teaching in recent times on the importance of vision and goal setting. Many are getting a grip of this. However, it is very interesting in my teaching around the world, whenever I have taken the time to ask people for their financial goals most have no clearly written financial goal even though they wake up every morning and hit the road to go and make money.

**Why?**

Firstly because of their ignorance of the curse of poverty.

*You will be cursed in the city and cursed in the country. Your*
*basket and your kneading trough will be cursed. The fruit of your*
*womb will be cursed, and the crops of your land, and the calves of*
*your herds and the lambs of your flocks. Deuteronomy 28:16-18*

Secondly because this same spirit of poverty which hangs upon people justifies their present condition and wants to hold them so.

Thirdly because it is a goal people have but do not make primary. They desire to have financial supply but it isn't primary enough for them to clearly define how much. To some people, other goals are more paramount whereas you cannot have financial breakthroughs until you prioritise your financial vision.

Why you may ask?

Firstly because setting financial goals and vision is the first step towards developing an effective spending plan.

Secondly, without a clearly defined financial vision you may be dissatisfied with where you are, where your life is going and how you are using your resources.

Thirdly, without a defined vision every upheaval, occurrence, incidence will set you off in a new direction without thought to where you will end up.

Financial goals are intended to help you determine where your money will go. It is an expression or a way of saying, "I have a future and I can control it."

> "Money is not everything…but poverty is nothing." -
> **V Demont Wiverg**

Have a vision. Have a long term perspective of your finances. Look down the horizon. You must have the ability to think ten, 20 or 30 years down the road.

However you must also have the skills to clearly define your financial vision or goals in short, mid-term, mid-long term, and long term in order to establish your doings.

A short-term vision is a goal that typically takes between zero to two years to complete. These are usually extremely important as your bigger and longer goals will depend on the success of the shorter ones.

These goals are important because they build the base for your financial increase. We shall attach a financial plan at the end of this chapter for you to begin a step in this direction.

Your mid-term goals are goals that will take less than five years to complete. It may include coming out of certain debts as in credit card debts. You must see the paying up of your debt as a form of savings because you are cutting down on the amount of outgoings, particularly the ones that are interest based.

Mid-long term financial goals are goals that will take five to 15 years to become a reality. The length of the time may mean that you must make room for evolution and change because your financial condition may also change because of certain things that will happen along the way.

Lastly, long term personal financial goals are the ones that take from 16 years to a lifetime to achieve. They include the creation of wealth, the building of multi-generational wealth, the preparation of your children to handle the things you have achieved.

They are sometimes underscored by a certain amount you desire to have at a particular age. These goals and visions must be **SMART**.

**S** - Specific
**M** - Measurable
**A** - Achievable
**R** - Realistic
**T** - Time based

**S**pecific goal means in effect that you know the amount you want.

**M**easurable goal means you must not waffle over the amount you desire God to provide.

**A**chievable means - it is no use, at your current rate of income to fix an amount that is unrealistic. If you are already 45 and you have no chosen skill, you will hardly put together $1 million. You cannot be saying you want to be richer than Bill Gates.

To be able to overtake a man who already has $48 billion you might have to discover what no one else has ever discovered.

**R**ealistic means - age, time and the ability to compound the money may mean that your goals could have been unrealistic if you were targeting what someone else has.

**T**ime based - we have mentioned earlier one, short term, mid-term, long-mid term and long term goals. These are ways to make your vision and financial goals time based.

Let your daily actions and affirmations agree with the desires you have in your heart. Organise everything, from the least to the most important vision you have to be in situ with the vision you have financially.

As a person who desires the miracle of wealth transfer you must move financial vision and goals to become one of the top values you have.

Meditate and count the benefits and the finances God has provided for you daily.

*Praise the LORD, O my soul, and forget not all his benefits-*
*Psalm 103:2*

Organise your savings and your investments. Do this by investing monthly, yearly until you have no money worries.

Your money vision becomes clear as you begin to calculate your financial net worth by adding up your assets and deducting all the liabilities.

Remember that your net worth is not the number of properties you own but those properties less the mortgages and indebtedness on them.

It is only your net worth that can help you in the days of calamity. In order to make financial vision clear you probably need to answer the following questions:

**1.** What are you saving and investing monthly?

**2.** What percentage of your income is saved?

**3.** What is your monthly cost of living?

**4.** What is your annual cost of living?

**5.** How many years have you worked?

**6.** What is the amount you have accumulated so far?

**7.** What have you given to serve the Lord?

**8.** What have you given to serve other people?

Your financial vision should include cutting down on your expenses in order to be debt-free, then spending quality time to read good books on finance.

Finally, you have to work smart. Give a greater percentage of your time to what pays more and the lesser percentage to things that are of lesser value.

## FINANCIAL VISION SHEET I

List some things you want that will require financial resources. If you are setting financial goals for the family, each family member should write a list of wants requiring financial resources.

### Things I Want That Require Money

1. _____ 5. _____
2. _____ 6. _____
3. _____ 7. _____
4. _____ 8. _____

### Short-Term Goals

Goals focus on what: what you need or what you want. Some goals you have listed can be achieved in two years or less. These goals are referred to as short-term goals.

From the list(s) you prepared, list the short-term goals. Be sure to combine the short-term goals of all family members.

### Financial goals that can be achieved in two years or less

_____

_____

_____

_____

_____

## Long-Term Goals

Long-term goals relate to what you want to accomplish in five or more years. Long-term goals usually require more resources for achievement. From your list(s) of wants, write down your long-term goals. Include the long-term goals of all family members.

**Financial goals to be achieved in five years or more**

_____

_____

_____

_____

_____

# FINANCIAL VISION SHEET II

**Purpose:** to identify personal financial goals and create an action plan.

**Instructions:** Based on personal and household needs and values, identify specific goals that require action.

**Short-term monetary goals (zero to less than two years)**

| Description | Amount Needed | Months to achieve | Action to be taken | Priority |
|---|---|---|---|---|
| e.g. pay off credit card debt | $1,000 | 12 | Use money from pay rise | High |
|  |  |  |  |  |
|  |  |  |  |  |
|  |  |  |  |  |
|  |  |  |  |  |
|  |  |  |  |  |

## Intermediate and long-term monetary goals

| Description | Amount Needed | Months to achieve | Action to be taken | Priority |
|---|---|---|---|---|
|  |  |  |  |  |
|  |  |  |  |  |
|  |  |  |  |  |
|  |  |  |  |  |
|  |  |  |  |  |

## Non-monetary goals

| Description | Time frame | Actions to be taken |
|---|---|---|
| e.g. set up file for personal financial records and documents | Next 2-3 months | Locate all personal and financial records and documents; set up files for various spending, saving, borrowing categories |
|  |  |  |
|  |  |  |
|  |  |  |

# 3. YOUR FINANCIAL *VOLUME*

When do you have enough finance?

The best answer of course is, "When you have enough to carry out your vision and dreams of life, then you have enough. When you have enough to feel contented, then you have enough."

Oftentimes those who hold the view that believers should not seek to experience wealth will quote the scripture that says, "Godliness with contentment is great gain."

*But godliness with contentment is great gain. 1 Timothy 6:6*

However, they do not take the time to look at the word, 'contentment.' That word conveys the feeling of satisfaction, having enough, having reached the point where there is no more desire.

The American Heritage Dictionary of the English Language (4th Edition) defines contentment as the state of being contented or satisfaction. Thesaurus.com renders its synonyms as being: comfort, content, contentedness, ease, equanimity, fulfilment, gladness, gratification, peace, pleasure, repletion, satisfaction, and serenity.

To have anything different from this would therefore mean a lack of contentment and if this is what contentment means it means we have misinterpreted the word and taking it to mean, "Just accepting your lot."

Roget's New Millennium Thesaurus adds to it. It says the word 'contentment' means abundance, alleviation, amenity, cheer, cheerfulness, convenience, cosyness, creature comfort, enjoyment, exhilaration, gratification, happiness, luxury, opulence, peacefulness, pleasure, plenty, poise, quiet, relaxation, relief, repose, rest, restfulness, satisfaction, snugness, sucker, sufficiency, warmth and well-being.

There could be no more added to that to show clearly that the intention of the word contentment is the well-being of the believer.

It is with that that we approach the subject of financial volume.

What is your dream?

This can only be decided by you because you are the one who feels what is appropriate for your future. However, in making such decisions you must remember there are predators that would want to eat into your finances of the future.

These predators can be the economy, the taxation system, life's uncertainties, bad decisions you may have made or which others made concerning you.

Until your goals are set in volumes what you get could be below your expectation and you cannot complain because a goal you did not set is a goal you will not achieve.

Therefore, may I ask you to answer the following questions:

**1.** How much would you want to earn this year?

**2.** How much would you want to earn next year?

**3.** How much do you want to be earning five years from now?

**4.** What is your plan to earn this kind of money?

**5.** How much do you want to be worth when you retire?

**6.** How much would you have to earn to achieve the goal?

**7.** What is your financial plan for acquiring the goal?

**8.** What are the steps to be taken?

**9.** Have you listed them in order of priority?

**10.** What is your daily, weekly, monthly and yearly financial goal?

**11.** What is your short term, mid-term, long mid-term, and long term goal?

**12.** Where are the financial boundaries in your life which says, these are the things I cannot do for money?

# CONCLUSION

One of the most profound prophesies in the Old Testament speaks of the day when the wealth of the wicked will be transferred to the righteous. We see many instances where this became a reality. Corporate wealth was released for Israel from the hand of the Egyptians, making millionaires out of ex-salves.

The prophesy of Elisha took the nation from shortage to oversupply, while the battle of Jehoshaphat brought by three nations resulted in abundant supply that took three days to gather and carry away.

Individuals also experienced this anointing; Abraham possessed the blessing of the kings when he conquered them at Sodom. Mordecai had all the wealth of Prime Minister Haman transferred to him, and an illiterate shepherd boy called Joseph inherited the wealth of kings in Egypt. Each occasion revealed the purpose of God for the season. In Egypt the ex-salves needed the gold and silver to build the tabernacle in the wilderness.

As we draw close to the end of times and the coming of Christ, the Church will need all the resources it can lay hands on to effectively preach its message to this mess age. I am convinced that we are in springtime and are about to enter a season of wealth transfer when we will make a global impact using timely technology to preach the timeless truth.